PATTI AND DANNY TAYLOR

San Antonio Adventure Guide

Contents

1

Introduction

San Antonio is one of the most beautiful and unique cities in the United States. When you travel to San Antonio you will find a mixture of cultures that have blended over the past generations to produce a rich history that has been preserved in many historical sites, museums, and other venues featured in this book.

This book will provide a compilation of sights and sounds of the city with addresses for your GPS, in order to be able to easily compile your list of things to do or see in a logical manner.

There is a section on bargain adventures and places to stay that will be kind to your travel budget and provide fun activities and exciting places to go.

Although some activities will be free, others will have an admission cost, but we will give you details when available to us.

Downtown San Antonio

R Downtown San Antonio, the heart of the city, is dominated by the presence of the Alamo, although it may seem dwarfed by the surrounding hustle and bustle of the area. There is so much history contained in this mission that was originally established in 1718 as Mission San Antonio de Valero. To this date, it has been lovingly preserved for its rich history. It is most famously known for its 1836 Battle of the Alamo wherein 186 Texans gave their lives for the independence of the state, but the 300-year period surrounding this battle is vital to the understanding of why the Alamo is important to the state.

In visiting the Alamo, you will find 16 major areas of interest. Each area will have a person (docent) who is a volunteer and can answer any question you might have, as well as direct you to the different exhibits you specifically want to find. Docents are easy to spot because they will be dressed in period clothing, often carrying common items that were used during 18th and 19th-century daily life. So, feel free to approach them and they will be able to help with what you need.

Entry to Alamo Church is always free to the public, and whether you are by yourself or in a larger party, you can always be accommodated. The only requirement is that you reserve your timed entry ticket either through the official website or onsite at the Alamo Welcome Center. You may reserve an entry that is free, an audio-guided tour that is $9 (or $5 for trip students), or a guided tour that is $40 for adults and $30 for children.

The major areas of interest are:

The Alamo Church is also called a "Shrine to Liberty". This church, which was originally designed to be a Spanish mission, is the structure that most of us think of when we think about the Alamo.

The Living History Encampment is located behind the church. There you will find a complete re-enactment of the daily life of someone who lived at the time of the Texas Revolution. They will be wearing the clothing of the period and performing the duties that made their lives more comfortable. Some of the duties include fire-starting, taking care of their health, and maintaining their firearms.

Although some of the medical practices are similar to today, some of the "different" methods of the 1830s may surprise and shock you.

Plan to come on Friday, Saturday, or Sunday to see live re-enactments of the firing of flintlock weapons that were used at the Battle of the Alamo. These take place at 11:00 am or 2:00 pm and can be found on the Alamo Plaza.

Another demonstration of interest is the firing of the new

bronze cannon that fires 6-pound cannon balls. You will witness the many jobs of the cannon crew as they go through several steps to prepare the cannon to be fired.

Although the Alamo was originally built as a Spanish mission, over the 300 years of its active use it was controlled at different times by four countries...Spain, Mexico, Texas, the United States, and even the Confederacy during the Civil War.

There are several priceless exhibits that you will want to see such as William B. Travis' heavy gold ring with a cat's eye stone in the center. A rifle that once belonged to Davy Crockett is also on display as well as a gold snuff box which, after the Battle of San Jacinto was given to General Sam Houston by General Santa Anna. I believe there is a $5 charge to visit this area unless you have purchased a ticket for an audio-guided or guided tour.

When you walk through Calvary Courtyard, you will be able to observe six beautifully crafted bronze statues that depict major heroes of the Texas Revolution and the Battle of the Alamo. First, you will see General William B. Travis, who led the brave men at the Alamo and is remembered for his war cry "Victory or death". Next, you will see James Bowie, the co-commander of the Alamo, who fought bravely from his sickbed during the battle. Others who are depicted in the bronze figures are John William Smith, the first mayor of San Antonio who carried messages out of the Alamo, Juan Nepomuceno Seguin, who served valiantly during the Texas Revolution, and Susanna Dickinson and her daughter who were the only survivors of the Battle of the Alamo. They took shelter in the church and were later freed and able to tell the true story of the heroes of the Alamo.

Is the Alamo haunted?

As a result of the defenders' bodies being burned, dismembered, mutilated, and buried in mass graves in the area surrounding the Alamo after the famous battle, the area has been the source of many legends and sightings of apparitions that have appeared over the last 200 years. Even before this battle occurred, the area around Alamo Plaza had served as a cemetery for at least 1,000 bodies. City workers and construction workers have come across skulls and other bones many times while excavating and renovating the Alamo.

The first sighting of spirits at the Alamo was reported soon after the Battle of the Alamo when Santa Anna was captured near what is now the city of Houston. To avenge his capture, Santa Anna sent word for 1,000 men to go back to burn the Alamo. When the men approached, they were met by angry apparitions waving swords and screaming "Do not touch the Alamo!". The soldiers retreated and would not go back. Many believe this story, but some said it was monks from the mission trying to protect it from further destruction. Soon after this incident, however, more troops were sent back by a Colonel Sanchez who was tasked with destruction of the mission, and these troops were greeted by a tall, ghostly spirit who scared them away once again. No one was willing to return, and today the Monument to the Alamo (The Cenotaph) stands as a reminder of the souls that were lost that day.

Over time, the city of San Antonio bought the old mission and began using the old barracks and mission as a jail and police headquarters. Many prisoners reported seeing apparitions and hearing moaning coming from the rooftops. After watchmen and guards complained and refused to patrol after dark the jail was moved to an alternate location.

Still, to this day, there are reports from both visitors and city employees, of sightings near and on top of the old mission at all hours of the day and night. Some have seen hideous figures coming out of the walls of the Alamo or anxious spirits pacing back and forth on the roof. Other paranormal activities have been witnessed, such as explosions, screams and in the background, a trumpet playing "El Deguello", the Mexican bugle call that was played during the siege.

Briefly, here are more reportings of specters that have been seen frequently in the area:

- The spirit of a woman seen walking (floating) across Alamo Plaza is said to be one of two women who were struck by lightning in the 1700s. This woman died, but the other survived.
- There are many reports of a man dressed in clothing from the early 1800s walking along a road that leads to Nacog-doches. This man is believed to be the only deserter of the battle and when asked he replies that he is trying to get back to where he belongs.
- Possibly the only celebrity that has been seen in ghostly fashion at the Alamo is John Wayne, who portrayed Davy Crockett in the 1960s movie "The Alamo". He became insistent that the movie be as accurate as possible and visited the original site several times. Soon after he died, there began a series of sightings of John Wayne on the grounds, talking to other men who, given the way they are dressed, are presumed to be the original defenders of the Alamo.

Today, the San Antonio area is deemed to be one of the most haunted areas in the United States. Other hotels and attractions will be pointed out in the remainder of this book. When you visit The Alamo and other historical sites of the city, you will have a good chance of going home with your own ghost story.

Visit 300 Alamo Plaza Call for reservations: 210/225-1391
FREE ADMISSION or Audio-Guided Tours - $9 Private Tours:
$30/children $40/adults

San Antonio Riverwalk

If you stroll just a few yards from the Alamo to the San Antonio
Riverwalk, or Paseo del Rio, you will find another treasure to
explore. This 15-mile trail, located just a few feet below street
level, is a peaceful, serene pathway that intertwines through
interesting parts of the city. What you will experience is almost
magical as you discover the feel of this beautiful city with so
much history, culture, and charm. The Riverwalk was born out
of necessity after a category 1 hurricane brought severe flooding
to the city of San Antonio in the 1920s causing much damage
to the downtown area and killing over 50 people. A young
architect, Robert H. H. Hugman is credited with the brilliant idea
of harnessing the river with a series of pathways and bridges
that could control flooding. His design followed in the footsteps
of the French Quarter in New Orleans, trying to preserve the
Spanish heritage of the area.

His original vision called for the addition of small shops,
dining establishments, and other points of interest along the
way. Although some improvements were made in the following
years, the project did not take off until 1968 when the World's
Fair came to San Antonio and small businesses began building
along the Riverwalk, bringing great success and prosperity to

the area.

Now, let's explore some of the most popular and interesting things to do along the Riverwalk.

Riverboat Dining Excursions – To do this, you must plan well ahead and contact the specific restaurant which you want to cater your affair. This is the perfect way to celebrate with your family, to entertain customers or groups of any size. The restaurant will then charter a boat and help you schedule your event. Take a leisurely sail down the river while enjoying your favorite meal.

River Boat Cruises – You may book a river boat cruise through "Go Rio" by visiting their website, or you may hop aboard at one of the 3 boarding points along the river. The tours are available any day of the year and they last about 30-40 minutes as they tour the river and the downtown area.

The cost of the river cruises are $13.50 for adults and $7.00 for children (ages 1-5). Senior citizens and Military - $11.50, local residents of Bexar County - $10.50

Nightlife on the River – There are many amazing venues to visit after dark along the river. One favorite is The Bier Garten where German cuisine and beverages are served. Enjoy sauerkraut, sausages, and other authentic German foods, live music, and servers who are dressed in German attire. For a tasty margarita at the end of the day, the Naked Iguana Tequila Lounge is sure to please. Mad Dog British Pub, On the Bend Oyster Bar and Pub, and Maddy McMurphy's Irish Sports Bar all have live entertainment and are just a few of the amazing night spots you will find along the Riverwalk.

How about some authentic Tex-Mex food for some spicy appetite pleasers? Visit Rio Rio Cantina for breakfast, lunch, or dinner and enjoy their Daily Specials that are always served with a side of Riverwalk fun! You will also find favorites such as The County Line that serves amazing barbequed ribs, brisket, and chicken. How about Boudro's Texas Bistro, one of the most popular dining venues since 1986? You will love trying one of their specialties, such as guacamole made right at your table or a prickly pear margarita.

Here are some interesting facts that you might like to know about the Riverwalk:

The Riverwalk is approximately 1.5 miles long.

1. The main part of the river is only 3 – 4 feet deep in the downtown area.
2. There is no physical address associated with the RiverWalk, but a centrally located address would be at the Hard Rock Café, which is 111 West Crockett Street.
3. The Riverwalk is only one or two blocks from the Alamo.
4. The Riverwalk never closes. Feel free to walk at any time, although the cafes and bars have set hours of operation.
5. Individuals do not need a reservation to ride on a River Boat. You may purchase tickets and hop on at either of 3 locations: the Aztec Theater, Rivercenter Mall, and across from the Palacio del Rio Hotel.
6. To park, you may find one of over 10,000 parking spots downtown. You will find surface lots, parking garages, and parking meters readily available.
7. You may hail a River Shuttle at any time by grabbing the driver's attention and they will pull over at the next dock to pick you up. A 1-Day Pass is $19.
8. There is a venue for weddings called Marriage Island, perfectly located on a peninsula behind the Contessa Hotel.

Please contact the City of San Antonio Parks and Recreation to book a wedding.

9. Celebrate with the City of San Antonio for the Christmas/Holiday parade on the Friday following Thanksgiving at 7:00 pm.

The Irish Flats

Both Irish and German immigrants arrived in San Antonio around the middle of the 19th century. Two hundred Irish Catholic families had settled farther south in Texas, near the present-day town of Sinton, but had moved to the San Antonio area after suffering several massacres in which many were killed. Their community, the Irish Flats, was located just a few blocks from Alamo Plaza, and there are just a couple of the original homes left standing today. This area is just north of the Alamo with Broadway as the boundary on the west, and the Acequia Madre as the boundary on the east. The unique homes that were built by the Irish immigrants were influenced by the style they had left in Ireland, blended with Spanish architecture along with German details. They featured thatched roofs with low roof lines and front porches that were narrow. This specific kind of home was known to be the only original architectural style in San Antonio. The stone used for the homes was procured from a quarry near Mission Concepcion.

As the city expanded around 1917, most of this area was demolished to make way for newer and more modern buildings, along with Hwy. 281 and Interstate 37. In the downtown area, you can still see several original homes that have been restored. You can walk by 127 McCullough Ave. and see the Ross-Kennedy home that is used as a venue for special events. It has the characteristic low-sloped roof used in times gone by. Other incredible examples of the homes of that period can be seen at 305 N. Alamo Street, 35 E. Crockett St., and 417 8th Street, all built in the 1800s.

There is speculation as to why this area was called "Irish Flats". One theory is that it was originally called "The Flat" until an artist (Jose Arpa) named his painting of the area "Irish Flats". Another story has it that since British and Irish folks call apartments "flats", that is where the name was derived.

San Antonio Missions

San Jose Mission

Of course, the most famous mission in the city is the Alamo, but there are several more that have a rich history and beautiful grounds begging you to visit. The San Jose Mission, formally named Mission San Jose y San Miguel de Aguayo, was built in 1720, with its location just south of the Alamo. You must visit the San Jose Visitor Center where a movie is featured that explains an overview of mission life. The mission still holds a bilingual weekly church service entitled Mariachi Mass.

One of the most intriguing examples of architecture from the Spanish colonial period is the Rose Window. The Rose Window is located just above the sacristy and is a magnificent piece of art. There is a mystery as to who actually crafted this masterpiece, but it is believed that Pedro Huizar (according to one account) was the artisan and he named it after his girlfriend who died during her voyage from Spain.

For easy access to all of the missions there is a 15-mile trail that can be either hiked or biked and will take you to each of the missions. There are approximately 2.5 miles between each mission. Admission is free and there are guided tours led by park rangers that are very informative and provide lots of detail about the history of each mission.

San Jose Mission: 6701 San Jose Drive, San Antonio, Tx., 78214

Mission Conception is a true testimony to a bygone era. Since there has been no restoration process applied here, when you visit this mission, you will see it as it appeared over two centuries ago. When it was first built, the lime plaster-covered walls were covered in brightly colored geometric designs, but these have faded away and are no longer visible. Unlikely as it may seem, there are several rooms that have original frescos (a type of wall art) visible to visitors. This mission is located at 807 Mission Road.

Mission Concepcion: 807 Mission Road, San Antonio, Tx., 78210

Mission San Juan Capistrano was built in East Texas but was moved to San Antonio in 1731 where it was originally used as a cemetery. When you walk along the trail beside the mission today, you will see a lot of the vegetation, the way it is shaded, and how the riverbank appears very much as it did over 300 years ago. Beginning in the mid-1700s this mission became a producer of agriculture and grew crops such as corn, sweet potatoes, squash, beans, and sugar cane by using an irrigation system in the fields. The mission also grew grapes, melons, peppers, and pumpkins and had around 3500 sheep and head of cattle. The residents started a network of villages, missions, and settlements to trade their abundance of produce and feed many settlers.

Mission San Juan: 9101 Graf Road, San Antonio, Tx., 78214

Mission Espada was the first mission built in Texas in 1690 and eventually moved to the San Antonio location around 1756. The desire of the Spanish missionaries was to make everyday life in the mission as close as possible to the daily life in Spanish villages. Native Americans were expected to learn the skills and traditions of Spain in order to become Spanish citizens. They learned weaving, blacksmithing, carpentry, and masonry, to name a few. Many of the skills learned by the Native Americans are embedded in the artisanry visible in the city today.

Demonstrations on Tuesday afternoons depict the weaving of sheep's wool by the same process that was used at the early mission.

Mission Espada: 10040 Espad Road, San Antonio, Tx., 78214

Tower of the Americas

The Tower of the Americas was specifically built in 1968 as part of the Hemisfair World's Fair celebrating the 250-year anniversary of the City of San Antonio. *A little-known fact: Suggestions were requested of the citizens of the city as to what material the tower should be built out of. One popular suggestion was beer cans. Yes, because of the popularity of the Pearl Brewery and other breweries in town, this was seriously considered.

Standing a Texas-sized 750 feet in the air, when you reach the top you will have a spectacular view from the (indoor and outdoor) Observation Deck that reveals the beauty of the city. This was the tallest structure in the United States after 1968, until the Stratosphere Tower in Las Vegas was built in 1996. Your ticket to the tower will also include a thrilling entertainment at the 4D theater show entitled "Skies Over Texas". You have access to dining at the Chart House Restaurant, the Tower Café, and Bar 601. The Charter serves delicious seafood and steaks and revolves around the tower as you dine.

This massive tower took two years to build and weighs over 80 million pounds with 952 steps leading to the top, but it will only take you 43 seconds when you ride one of the three elevators that can carry 1,950 visitors per hour.

<u>739 Tower of the Americas Way, San Antonio, Tx., 78205</u>

The tickets are $16.50 for adults and $12.00 for children under 12. Children under the age of 3 are free, with discounts for seniors and military personnel.

3

The San Antonio Zoo

Y ou will want to set aside at least 3-4 hours (preferably in the morning) to visit this zoo that was opened in 1929 with a grant from the wealthy Brackenridge family. It is located on a sprawling 56 acres and houses more than 8,500 animals, including a bird sanctuary that is one of the largest in the world. This birdhouse permits the birds to fly freely in an area that simulates a tropical rainforest. More than one million visitors pass through its gates every year to enjoy the animals. It is the zoo's mission to teach conservation and the preservation of wildlife, and to instill this desire in others. Among the inhabitants of the zoo, you will find those that are endangered or may be extinct in the wild.

Included in a "Fun Day" ticket to the zoo are several attractions that you should check out, and this should start with the new Selva 4D Theater. The sensory special effects such as snow, wind, seat vibrations, scent, and special FX lighting will immerse guests in a family-friendly movie experience.

Other special adventures available are Flamingo Mingle, Behind the Scenes: Hippos, Behind the Scenes: Okapi, a VIP

Walking Tour, Kangaroo Krossing, Zootennial Carousel, and the Zoo Train.

The zoo offers adventures at breakfast, featuring a huge choice of breakfast foods and the opportunity to feed some of the zoo animals. Take your choice of giraffes, kangaroos, or hippos and have your picture taken as the zoo specialist teaches you about each animal with his interesting presentation.

Perhaps the ultimate zoo experience can be found in the Lory Landing, which is the home of the lorikeets – small, brightly colored, and gregarious parrots. They will delight you by performing such behaviors as hanging upside down or dancing. They consume nectar which you may purchase by the cupful at the nearby Lory Café. What a fun and exciting experience for all ages!

3903 N. St. Mary's St., San Antonio, Tx., 78212 / Phone: 210/734-8184

Adults: $31.99 Children 3-11: 29.99 Children under 3: FREE (Check for discount codes when buying tickets on line)

4

Six Flags Fiesta Texas

Originally named Fiesta Texas, this theme park was built in 1992 with the purpose of becoming a destination musical show park that would feature the musical culture of the state of Texas. It was bought by Time Warner in 1995 and became a 6 Flag theme park in 1996.

One of the most popular attractions is the "Scream" ride which is easy to spot from all areas of the park. This ride is brightly colored and stands over 200 feet tall.

Six Flags Fiesta Texas is divided into seven areas and each boasts a different theme. White Water Bay is the name of the water park located adjacent to these areas.

Along with the "Scream", there are approximately 17 other rides designated as "thrill rides". The "Screamin' Eagle Zipline" ride is unique in that you may take a friend alongside you as you zip through the course.

You must be brave to approach "Batman: The Ride" as it is a newly designed free-fly roller coaster that has you flying and flipping over a twelve-story hill and then down two vertical drops. If you are looking for thrills, this ride has them coming and going, with special effects and a unique design. There are several family-friendly rides in the park. You might like to come down to the Fiesta Bay Boardwalk to ride on this 90-foot giant of a Ferris wheel. As you are slowly lifted to the top in a brightly colored gondola that is large enough for the whole family, you will be able to see a beautiful, panoramic view that stretches for miles in each direction.

Another example of the family-friendly rides found in the theme park is the Fiesta Texas Railroad. There is no minimum height to ride this classic locomotive. You can board at two different rail stations in the park and take a leisurely ride around the area.

There is an area specially designated for toddlers and children, filled with rides for the young ones. The Ramblin' Road lets them steer their own car, the Kinderstein is a spinning ride (if that's what they like), and the Pirate Ship Play Zone features a rope ladder, a slide, and a shaded area that provides relief from the sun. These are just a few of the many attractions in this area.

The water park comes with the general admission to Six Flags Fiesta Texas. In this water park are several water slides, a water coaster, a lazy river, several dining areas, and a shop where you can purchase sunscreen and other necessities. A smoking area is provided as well.

One of the first rides you will come to after entering the water park is the lazy river. You can grab one of the many inner tubes and have a calm and restful ride through the park. Big Bender and Whirlpool are the next rides you will come to. Just remember there is a weight limit for these 2 rides (250 pounds per individual or 400 pounds if you take the double innertubes). The Whirlpool slide reminds us of a toilet bowl swirling around and around.

There is an upper level to the park with many more attractions to choose from. The Texas Tumble, Bermuda Triangle, and Riptide Runner are a few examples of rides located in this area along with the Tidal Wave Café and a first aid station.

There are double-level cabanas that can be rented for about $500, but the cost can be split among a large group. They provide lots of privacy and a place rest and people watch when you are tired. In addition, they are equipped with small refrigerators, and food service is available to feed your group. All in all, this water park will provide lots of fun for visitors of all ages.

17000 W. I-10, San Antonio, Tx., / Phone: 210/697-5050

Online Day Tickets start at $59.99 (Annual Membership and Seasonal Passes also available)

5

Popular Restaurants

L *a Fogata*
This restaurant has been serving traditional Mexican cuisine to the citizens of San Antonio for over 35 years. The ambiance is that of a lush, tropical setting, with your choice of indoor or outdoor service. Featuring an award-winning salsa and tasty margaritas that have been voted "Best in San Antonio", they are known far and wide. Conveniently located in three different areas of town, you will most likely be near one of them during your stay in San Antonio.

2427 Vance Jackson Rd., San Antonio, Tx., /Phone: 210/340-1337

Mi Tierra

Pete and Cruz Cortez opened their little three-table café, known as Mi Tierra in San Antonio in 1941. Their goal was to serve breakfast not only to the farmers of the area, but to the early rising workers who went to work every day in the Mercado. Today, 60 years later, the Cortez family still owns the world-famous restaurant which has grown to seat a capacity of 500. Their goal is to carry on the tradition of serving the local residents as well as tourists from all over the world who come to visit San Antonio. Check this one out to get a taste of their authentic Mexican dishes as well as their genuine warm hospitality.

218 Produce Row, San Antonio, Tx., 78207 / Phone: 210/225-1262

La Fonda on Main

Having been established in 1938, this restaurant claims to be the oldest restaurant in San Antonio. You will find that they serve authentic Mexican dishes brought from the interior of Mexico, along with a splash of Tex-Mex. A quiet, shady outdoor patio may be to your liking, but perhaps you would be more comfortable in the cool hacienda-style dining room in the summer months. Try their special enchilada dinner, oak grilled fajitas or some of the more unique dishes that include pollo milanesa, camarones al ajillo, or diver scallops veracruzana. I think you will like any of these dishes.

22415 North Main Ave, San Antonio 78212 210-733-0621

The CommonWealth Coffeehouse & Bakery

This local favorite opened its doors in January 2015 in Alamo Heights. Located in a historic home that had been totally renovated, the owners wanted to operate an establishment that featured French breads and pastries made by French bakers in the traditional way. There are now four locations in the city of San Antonio where local residents along with visitors from all over the world can enjoy heavenly breakfast concoctions, such as the breakfast croissant bechamel or the breakfast tacos made with homemade tortillas filled with eggs cooked to the texture of French-style omelets.

In the blink of an eye this popular community gathering place can go from a calm atmosphere to being filled with a mixture of students from nearby Incarnate Word University, young professionals and women of all ages dressed in expensive workout gear.

118 Davis Ct., San Antonio, Tx., 78209 / Phone: 210/560-2955

Tito's Mexican Restaurant

Making Tito's restaurant casual and authentic has been the goal of Mark Rodriguez and sister, Denise Rodriguez. Mark traveled the interior of Mexico to find the most delicious and unique recipes for their family-owned establishment. Some examples of their specialty dishes include Tacos Pastor, Tacos Banados, and Puntas de Filete en chile Chipotle. Just check out their menu and see why their customers come back time and time again.

955 South Alamo Street, San Antonio 78205 / Phone: 210-212-8226

6

Hotels Near Downtown

he Mokara Hotel and Spa
The Mokara Hotel and Spa is very highly rated and is located just blocks away from the San Antonio Riverwalk. After you have spent the day downtown, come back here for cooling off in the pool or take time to visit the spa.

212 West Crockett Street, San Antonio, Tx 78205 210-396-5800 Rating 4.5 and Room Rates start at $319.00 (Seasonal Rates)

Hotel Havana
Hotel Havana is situated in the heart of the city, adjacent to the Tobin Center for Performing Arts on a quiet stretch of the North Riverwalk. It was built in 1934 and is known for its quaint yet elegant style and has been recognized in the National Register of Historical Places. All 27 rooms are decorated with antique furniture and feature the original Bastrop pine floors.

1050 Navarro Street, San Antonio, Tx 78205 210-222-2008 Rating 4.0 Room Rates start at $175.00 (Seasonal Rates)

The Westin Riverwalk
This modern, upscale hotel is nestled on the Riverwalk and within walking distance of the Pearl District, a unique destina-

tion which features downtown shopping, entertainment, bars and unique dining. Enjoy walking to the Spanish Governor's palace or the Alamo to take in the architecture of this historic period. Fiesta Texas and the Zoo are just a short drive away.

420 Market Street, San Antonio, Tx 78205 210-224-6500 Rating 8.6 out of 10 and Room Rates start at $229.00 (Seasonal Rates)

Hyatt Regency Riverwalk

This hotel opens up directly to the San Antonio Riverwalk and is just steps away from the Alamo and all the wonderful dining facilities, shopping areas, and entertainment that you will find in the charming heart of the city. You will be able to explore the missions and the King William District, where you can view restored as well as unrestored homes built in the 1800's in Victorian, Greek revival, and Italian styles. All this and much, much more is within walking distance.

123 Losoya Street, San Antonio, Tx 78205 210-222-1234 Rating 4.5 Room Rates start at $221.00 (Seasonal Rates)

Omni La Mansion del Rio

As indicated by the name, this beautiful hotel is located on the San Antonio River, just a 7-minute walk from the Alamo. You will be close to all the historic and cultural activities you can find in downtown San Antonio.

112 College Street, San Antonio, Tx 78205 210-518-1000 Rating 4.4 Room Rates start at $211.00 (Seasonal Rates)

Hotel Valencia

This hotel, originally built in 2003, has recently had a $10 million dollar face lift. It is conveniently located downtown, near Alamo Plaza. Interesting pieces of art are featured throughout the hotel including four cow skulls decorated in black and white mosaic print.

150 East Houston Street, San Antonio, TX 78205 855-596-3387
Rating 4.3 Room Rates start at $179.00 (Seasonal Rates)

St. Anthony Hotel - San Antonio

This grand hotel, on the list of National Historic Landmarks, has been restored to its original elegance and charm. This most cherished and favored hotel of the city was built in 1909, claiming the title of the most luxurious hotel in Texas. It fell into ruin during the depression but was successfully renovated and re-opened in 1983. Many famous people have stayed at the St. Anthony including several Presidents, Vice Presidents, actors, and actresses. It is located downtown, close to all the favorite sights of the city.

Does the St. Anthony Hotel have a ghost story? It has been reported many times that guests and employees have seen shadowy figures come and go and have experienced sudden and drastic temperatures changes inside the hotel. But the answer to the question is, even though we do not know the specific names of the ghosts, there are quite a few that have been seen over and over again.

First on the list of reported ghostly figures is the "Lady in Red" who appears entering the women's bathroom. She apparently needs go really badly as she scurries across the tile flooring in her red dress, making clip clop noises in her heels. Guests report she enters the first stall and then, as they peer under the door, her feet and legs vanish right before their eyes, never to be seen again. Perhaps, legend says, she was staying at the hotel, ran into the bathroom, but began to have a heart attack and quickly ran back to her guest room where she eventually died. No one knows for sure, but many ARE sure that they have seen her.

The tenth floor which was added on to the hotel during the Depression is noted to be the floor with the most paranormal activity. Many bellmen claimed to have heard the shuffling of feet behind them as they walked down the hallway, but each time they turned around to look, no one was following them.

There is another spirit that haunts this floor that appears as a tall man dressed in a dark suit who rides the elevator to the tenth floor , steps out into the hallway, and suddenly disappears from sight.

For the most chilling story of the St. Anthony, please read the story that begins in the Gunter Hotel and ends at the St. Anthony. It involves Room 536 and is a true-life crime story that does not end well. But don't worry...room 536 no longer exists as it was split into two rooms during renovations.

300 E. Travis Street, San Antonio, Tx 78205 210-227-4392
Rating 4.5 Room Rates start at $465.00 (Seasonal Rates)

Menger Hotel

This historic hotel was built in 1859 on Alamo Square, just adjacent to the Alamo. It went through good times and bad times and eventually fell into disrepair. Finally in 1945, after World War II, it was revitalized, many improvements were made, and the Menger was recognized as a landmark once again. The hotel has housed many important guests, including Presidents from Grant to Roosevelt to Clinton. This is certainly a grand hotel, worth visiting to see it in its splendid state once again.

The Menger Hotel also has the distinction of being one of San Antonio's haunted attractions. Being near the Alamo, it is believed that some of the heroes who died in that battle walk the halls of this old hotel.

There seem to be as many as 32 entities that call the Menger home from time to time. Among the most famous is Teddy Roosevelt, who would occasionally frequent the bar, casually offering a free drink to unsuspecting cowboys just off the Chisolm Trail. Some would find themselves the next day, headed to Ft. Sam Houston, signed up as a recruit to help fight the Spanish American War. So, Teddy Roosevelt can be seen sitting at the bar enjoying one last drink. Another ghostly spirit is that of Sally White, a chambermaid who was killed in the hotel by an abusive husband. Her spirit continues to go about her duties carrying fresh towels down the hallways of the Victorian wing of the Menger.

Captain Richard King, one time the owner of the largest ranch in the world (The King Ranch in South Texas), was a frequent visitor to the Menger. He spent his last months in the hotel and eventually died there. His funeral was held in the hotel parlor. Today, he is often seen entering through the walls of what is now called "The King Ranch Room", exactly where the door was before renovations. None of these entities seem to mind sharing the hotel with the living and remain friendly to employees and guests.

204 Alamo Plaza, San Antonio, Tx 78205 210-223-4361 Rating 4.4 Room rates start at $159.00 (Seasonal Rates)

The Crockett Hotel

Named after the legendary Davy Crockett of Alamo fame, this historic hotel was built just steps away from Alamo Plaza in 1909. It was expanded in 1927 when the vast west wing was added. In 1982, the present owner restored the original architectural design elements that make it unique and charming today.

Because of its proximity to the Alamo, the hotel has a reputation for being one of the most haunted hotels in the area. Whispers which seem to come from the hallways are believed to be the voices of Davy Crockett and the other defenders of the Alamo, as they discuss unfinished business from centuries before. One employee reportedly saw the sensory-operated front door open to let in an unseen visitor. No living soul was anywhere near the door.

One of the most actively haunted areas of the Crockett Hotel is the Executive Office, located in the exact spot where Santa Anna's troops stood at the last siege.

Employees have witnessed the opening and closing of curtained windows, knowing that no one was the room. Visitors have been surprised to see colorful orbs in photographs taken in the lobby or guest rooms. Most folks who actually encounter a ghost in the bar or lobby say that it is a man dressed in a dark blue uniform, likely that of a Texas Revolution soldier.

Visit the Crockett, only 18 steps away from the Alamo, for an event-filled vacation in San Antonio.

320 Bonham St., San Antonio, Tx. Phone: 210/225-6500

Room Rates: Start at $130

The Emily Morgan Hotel

Based on the history of this hotel, I would be shocked if it was NOT haunted. This beautiful building in the heart of Downtown San Antonio originally served as a medical building (Medical Arts), housing a hospital and doctor's offices. First built in the 1920s, it was eventually sold to be used for office space and then again in 1982 when it was converted into the luxury hotel it remains today.

Over the years it has been recognized for its historical value and has received awards for its unique Gothic Revival architectural design. Perhaps the most interesting award it received was in 2015 when it was identified as being the third most haunted hotel in the world.

It has been noted by guests and hotel employees over the years, that the fourteenth, the ninth, and the seventh floors appear to have the most paranormal activity. These were the floors that housed the psychiatry department and ward, the operating rooms, and the hospital morgue.

If you are staying on one of these floors, you might expect to smell hospital odors, or you could feel a sudden temperature change, as if walking into a refrigerated area.

In particular, the floor that seems to generate a lot of mystery is the fourteenth floor. In addition to the overwhelming smell of a hospital in general, guests have been surprised to open their guest room door to the hall and see the scene of a waiting room filled with people. Upon second glance, this scene would disappear.

It appears the 12th floor has spirits that are playful at times, often opening and closing doors in the middle of the night. Guests have reported being awakened by the sound of a dripping faucet only to enter the bathroom and find the spigots opened to a full rush of water. When guests approach the sink, the water turns completely off by itself. Perhaps the creepiest vision is that of apparitions dressed in nurses uniforms, noisily pushing patients on wobbly gurneys down the hallways and then vanishing without a trace as quickly as they appeared.

Even though strange things happen on the afore mentioned floors, some of the scariest experiences take place when guests on the elevator are whizzed past the first floor and into the basement (which originally housed the hospital's morgue). The basement area is not normally accessible to the general public or guests, but employees who have had to perform repairs or other duties in the basement have seen strange things such as floating, colorful orbs of light and have heard voices when there was no one else present.

In the early days, it seems as though this basement area was also used as a crematorium and, needless to say, the air in the basement still carries the unpleasant smell of that process from long ago. So, if you get caught in the elevator as it lurches down to the basement area, do not get off! Just push the button that says "Lobby" and jump off there.

The Menger Hotel

7

Brackenridge Park

T here is so much to see at Brackenridge Park, we wonder - where shall we start? Let's begin with one of the most popular attractions linking many areas of the park together. That would be the San Antonio Zoo train, a miniature replica of a train from 1863. The train will take you on a 2-mile journey, stopping at various get-off points, including the Zoo, the Witte Museum, and the Japanese Tea Garden. The Zoo Train has an interesting story of its own as it was involved in the last armed train robbery, dubbed "The Great (Little) Train Robbery", in the state of Texas in 1970. Don't worry, this was over 50 years ago when several armed and masked men approached the train and demanded every one turn over their wallets and cash. The last known train robbery prior to 1970 was committed 47 years earlier at the end of the Wild West era.

3910 North St. Mary's St. San Antonio, Tx. Train ride is $4 for adults, Children FREE!
Witte Museum
Another popular destination as you ride the train around the 2-

mile track in Brackenridge Park is the Witte Museum. If you are interested in Texas history, Texas culture or the natural sciences of the Southwest, you must visit the Witte Museum. It has many interesting parts for adults and children alike. Since its opening in 1926, hundreds of thousands of school children and families have visited the Witte each year to explore the wonders hidden in their exhibits.

The Witte's 10-acre campus lies along the banks of the San Antonio River just below the headwaters. It is filled with ancient specimens of petrified rock from bygone eras as far back as the Cretaceous period, as well as artifacts from Archaic times. One notable exhibit features the Acequia Madres (an ancient agricultural irrigation system), built in 1719 to use water from the river during the Spanish period.

Over the years the Witte has grown from a small collection of natural history specimens to a sprawling campus with many different areas housing interesting and exciting exhibits. In the 1930s the museum added archaeological specimens from research conducted in the Big Bend area of Texas, and a Reptile Garden which benefitted the museum with added revenue and helped the Texas ranchers and workers who collected and sold rattlesnakes and other kinds of snakes for display at $0.10 - $0.15 per pound.

In the 1940's, two historic homes of San Antonio were moved to the Witte campus to provide additional room for expanding the exhibits.

1960 brought in the McFarlin Jewel Room which is famous for a diamond heist in 1968. A 49.73 carat canary diamond, valued at $365,000, was snatched from its resting place in a prominent display by a man who came into the Jewel Room carrying a lawn chair. When the security guard went to lunch, the man shattered the display, ran to the exit, and blocked the escape route with his lawn chair. Eventually, the diamond was recovered in New York and re-purchased by the McFarlin family in San Antonio. In addition to being very wealthy, some of the members of the McFarlin family were known to be quite eccentric. One McFarlin used to take his pet duck riding in the front seat of his Rolls Royce and while visiting clubs in the area, he would leave his duck sitting on the top of the bar as he frequented the dance floor.

The 1980s and 1990s saw further expansion of the exhibits offered at the Witte, and in 2003 the Herzberg Circus Collection became the newest addition when it was moved from the San Antonio Public Library. This collection was considered one of the largest of circus memorabilia including programs, manuscripts, journals, sheet music, and photographs.

Some of the most interesting exhibits currently available for view at the Witte include the McLean Family Texas Wild Gallery, the Naylor Family Dinosaur Gallery and Dinosaur Lab. The "New Witte" was welcomed in 2017, with many upgrades to the exhibits and a new entry and expanded lobby area featuring replicas of a fierce *Tyrannosaurus rex*, an *Acrocanthosaurus atokensis*, and a *Quetzalcoatlus* suspended from the ceiling and showing off its 40-foot wingspan.

Two captivating exhibits currently available for viewing at the Witte are "The Power of Poison" and "Fiesta Vogue: Outfits of the Day". "Power of Poison" is set against the backdrop of a Columbian rainforest. You will find many poisonous things that could harm you or could heal you. Among the vines of the rainforest are poisonous caterpillars, frogs and plants. Learn how local plants and animals, including rattlesnakes, monarch butterflies and poison ivy, have a role in the adaptation of poison for good or bad. Many are being used in research for new drugs for healing.

"Fiesta Vogue: Outfits of the Day" is much more serene and depicts the style of Fiesta. Whether they are the Royal Robes of Fiesta or the iconic street styles, they are fascinating. These exhibits change frequently, but there is always something new to be experienced.

3801 Broadway, San Antonio, Texas Admission: $14-Adults $13-Seniors $10- Children 12 and under

Japanese Tea Garden

Another experience connected to Brackenridge Park, The Japanese Tea Garden, also known as the Sunken Garden, was crafted in an existing limestone quarry in the early 1900s. This quarry originally supplied limestone for many of the unique structures around early San Antonio, including the Menger Hotel. Early city leaders obtained donors to fund a project that used prison inmates to craft the quarry into a visual paradise that included walkways, a Japanese pagoda, arched bridges made of stone, and an island.

The gardens changed names several times around World War II, as Japanese sentiment was negative for many years. After years of neglect and lack of funding, it came close to being closed permanently, but residents came to its rescue and the original name was restored. Improvements were made with bond funding and the pagoda and waterfall areas were restored to their former beauty and charm. This is the perfect place to go and enjoy the serenity and peace on a busy, bustling day in the city.

3853 North St. Marys Street, San Antonio, Tx 78212 210-212-4814 Admission: FREE FOR ALL AGES

8

More Downtown Sights To See

L*a Villita*

La Villita, or "little village", began as a cornerstone of the City of San Antonio more than 300 years ago. Over this span of ages, this area has evolved to become an integral part of the history and culture of the area and is now known as "La Villita Historic Arts Village".

In the beginning, the villagers of this area had no legal ownership of the land they occupied. The borders of this village were what is now the Alamo to the north and adjacent to the San Antonio River. It was near the Presidio San Antonio de Bejar, so it was protected from enemies and served as a secure place to peacefully raise crops, their animals and their families.

At the beginning of the 19th century the surrounding missions and the La Villita area came together to form what is now the City of San Antonio. There was little stability in the area over the next few decades, with the threat of invasion looming over the resident's heads. The most prevalent groups or cultures during this period were the Americans, the Mexicans, and the Germans. In addition, slaves and those of English, Irish and

French descent also lived in the area.

Over the years, the area of La Villita declined and, let's face it...It became a slum with the City of San Antonio growing up around it. But in 1926, the mayor of San Antonio decided that the La Villita area had a future and should be restored and serve as a monument to the hard working people who settled this land and went through years and years of hardship to bring the many cultures of the area together.

Today, La Villita has been transformed into a magical, one square block that is home to over 25 artisan shops where you may visit such establishments as art galleries featuring original art, and goods, gifts, and accessories handmade by local artisans. There is at least one original adobe home that has been renovated, with other buildings rebuilt to reflect the Victorian and Texas vernacular limestone structures of the 19th century.

At any given time of the year, you may be treated to one of over 200 special events held in this little village neighborhood.

With such an interesting and OLD history, you might wonder if this small area is resident to any ghosts? Well, of course it is! The stories and legends abound, and you will be astounded at the number that are well documented in this tiny area of downtown. Even if you are not a ghost hunter, you are likely to encounter one. Along with the Alamo, the Menger Hotel, and the Spanish Mansion, La Villita is one of the most active sites for a paranormal experience. In fact, La Villita could be considered one of the most haunted areas in San Antonio, or the state of Texas.

Three little shops on Villita Street, one a jewelry store and the other two art galleries, have had strange happenings over the years. The have all had objects move around, whispers heard when no one was there and they all have the spirit of a woman, seemingly trapped on the earth by some unknown force. All three women are dressed differently. One is wearing an apron, one is wearing pioneer garb, and the last one is wearing all white clothing.

The ghost of a little girl seems to be trapped in La Villita house (the Gissi House), built by a man named Cirilus Gissi. He was said to have buried gold under his house, but none was ever found. But people have seen an active little girl who may have been this man's granddaughter.

Some of the scarier ghost stories involve beheaded ghosts who are actually looking for their head (or anyone's head for that matter). These could be just the scary legends told around campfire to send a jolt to the children, so they won't go sneaking off in the middle of the night. Or they could be based on the ghoulish activities that actually happened back in the days of the wild west in San Antonio.

418 Villita St. San Antonio, TX 78205

San Fernando Catholic Church (also known as the Cathedral of Our Lady of Candelaria and Guadalupe)

This church (Roman Catholic) is located in Downtown San Antonio and is recognized as one of the earliest cathedrals built in the United States.

The exact date of the original building is not known but it is believed to have been constructed between 1738 and 1750 by those coming to the United States from the Canary Islands. The original walls of that church remain as the outer walls of the sanctuary today.

During the years surrounding the Battle of the Alamo, Jim Bowie was married in this church. It was taken over by Santa Anna and his soldiers as the siege of the Alamo took place and that is where he hung the flag that was marked "no quarter", meaning "complete destruction of the enemy, without mercy". It is believed that when the ashes of the men that died at the Alamo were recovered, they were given burial at the San Fernando Catholic Church. In addition, during the early years of the church, many parishioners, regardless of their station in life, were buried within the wall of the church. It is thought by many that much of the paranormal activity seen at the church is generated by the souls buried within or under its walls.

Several times, as guided tours were being conducted at the cathedral, a man dressed in black 17th century period clothing was spotted following the group and eventually disappearing, seemingly into thin air. *Other sightings involve apparitions that appear to be monks who may have been buried there long ago,* and the fact that tourists often spot ghost-like figures in the courtyards have piqued the interest of paranormal investigators. Visit this beautiful example of the long history of San Antonio and enjoy either a self-guided or a guided tour.

115 Main Plaza, San Antonio, Tx. 78205 Phone: 210/227-1297

King William Historic District

This area is a neighborhood bordered by the San Antonio River, Caesar Chavez Blvd., South St. Marys Street, and South Alamo Street. This area is believed to have been named for Wilhelm I, King of Prussia. One of its first early settlers was Carl Guenther, who built his home and mill in this neighborhood in 1859. The Guenther House still stands today and can be seen from the Mission Trails hiking or biking trail. The area continued to grow until the early 1900's when the homes became bigger and grander. The architectural styles varied from home to home and included classical revival style, colonial revival, Queen Anne and Romanesque. Some of these homes are now open to the public as museums in this neighborhood.

The Gunter Hotel

This historic hotel, in downtown San Antonio was opened in 1909 and was eventually bought by the Sheraton Hotel group. It has a very colorful history and mysterious past. The current property on which the Gunter Hotel sits has been the site of previous hotels since 1837. Originally, it was an eight-story building, named for Jot Gunter, one of its financiers and a local property owner. It has been enlarged over the years and in 1980-1985 was restored to some of its former glory.

In 2007 the Gunter Hotel was recognized for its historical significance and named to the U.S. National Register of Historical Places. In addition to being known for its early beginnings and historic value, it is also perceived by many as a place to experience paranormal adventures. Many people report seeing ghosts of the defenders of the Alamo and experiencing sudden drops in temperature that leave your body feeling chills up and down your spine. In addition, people sometime feel as if they are being watched, only to find no one there when they turn around. This feeling might persist over and over until you lock your room door behind you.

As many patrons of the hotel have reported, there are two ghostly women who haunt the halls and bicker back and forth with each other, possibly challenging each other for control. It seems as though they are thought to be either flappers or prostitutes who died during the 1920's. They even have names – Peggy and Ingrid.

There is a longstanding unsolved murder mystery that happened in 1965 at the Gunter Hotel. It seems as though a man calling himself Albert Knox registered and was seen for several days entering Room 636 with a tall woman at his side. A few days later, when a maid entered the room, she observed Mr. Knox holding a bloody sheet and standing in a room covered in blood spatter. He ran out the door, past the maid as she called for help. When police arrived, they found the bedroom and bathtub covered with sticky blood, but no body was found. Mr. Knox disappeared and the mystery surrounding the missing body was never solved. When a man fitting Mr. Knox's description checked in months later at the St. Anthony Hotel and asked for Room 636, the police were called. As they arrived and knocked at the door of Room 536 (636 had not been available), they heard a gunshot and found the occupant had committed suicide.

One more twist to the story...Only 10 years ago, a piece of mail was delivered to the general manager of The Gunter Hotel (not the Sheraton Gunter Hotel), with a date stamp of 1965. It contained a key to Room 636 and was the type of key used in that era. Many visitors to the hotel have seen a replay of a violent occurrence played out in the hall near Room 636 and paranormal investigators believe that it is the imprint of the murder that happened in 1965. Don't worry, when you check in to the Gunter, you will find that the infamous Room 636 has been renovated and split into 2 rooms now.

205 E. Houston St. San Antonio, TX 78205 Room Rates Start $209

210/227-3241

Spanish Governors' Palace

In the early 18th century, the French and the Spanish had a fierce rivalry for control of what is now the Southwestern area of the United States. In order to make sure the French did not invade this area, King Philip V of Spain ordered that there was to be built a mission built near San Pedro Creek and the San Antonio River headwaters. This structure was near the site of the present-day Alamo and was named Presidio San Antonio de Bejar. The original structure remained until 1722 when the Governor of Coahuila and Texas abandoned it and moved it to its present location. It was used as various venues over the years, including saloons, a tire shop, and a pawn shop until 1915 when one of Texas' first preservationists realized that the crumbling old building across the street from City Hall was actually one of the last remnants of the Spanish Texas era and needed to be saved and restored. In 1928, the city bought and began the restoration of this structure, which resulted in a bigger, grander interpretation of the original complex. It now stands as a museum in the heart of the city and represents the oldest era of San Antonio de Bejar.

105 Plaza de Armas, San Antonio, Tx 78205 210-207-7527 Admission-60 years, Military ID and Children under 7 - $3.00, Adults $5.00

9

San Antonio Museums

San Antonio Museum of Art

Downtown San Antonio hosts in the historic Lone Star Brewery building one of the most interesting attractions in the city – San Antonio Museum of Arts (SAMA). You will find a wealth of information that covers 5,000 years of world history and culture. After the brewery had been renovated to a tune of over $7 million, this super attraction opened to be viewed by the public in 1981.

Since 1926, and formerly housed in the Witte Museum, a great number of natural history objects and works of art became too much to stay in that location, especially after 1970 when the Witte was gifted beautiful collections from artists such as Wayne Thiebaud, Frank Stella, and Philip Guston. It was suggested that the complex known as the Lone Star Brewery be purchased and all the art acquisitions be moved to that location. A more perfect spot could not have been found, and it now serves as the entrance to the "Museum Reach" portion of the Riverwalk.

You will be amazed to see, as you walk through this museum, over 30,000 examples collected from all over the world—antiquities from Greek and Roman cultures, art from Asia, art from present day, and art from Latin America.

Among its largest collections, the museum hosts many pieces of art from the Roman, Greek and ancient Egyptian cultures and is said to be the largest in the southern United States.

Included in the Egyptian collection are objects from as far back as the pre-dynastic era. There is also, from the Roman and Greek exhibit, an unusual collection of sculptures which includes subjects from Greek mythology, portraits, and memorials.

In 2005, a grand 15,000 square foot gallery was added to support the growing Asian Art collection, which consists of over 1,500 pieces of art and is considered to be one of the largest in the United States. This impressive collection comes from all over the world, including countries such as Korea, India, Laos, Nepal, Sri Lanka, Japan, and others.

If you are interested in art from Latin American, this museum is pleased to present to you one of the most extensive collections in the United States. Within the walls of the Nelson A. Rockefeller Center for Latin American Art, you will find selections of art from Mexico and South and Central America, as well as 7,000 items representing Latin American folk art.

To represent Contemporary Art, you will find local San Antonio artists who, along with others, are featured from the year 1960 until now in the unique Texas Art Collection. Other contemporary works come from paintings and sculptures from World War II until the present.

There are always special exhibits at SAMA and this summer one of the featured exhibits is "Tony Parker's Heroes and Villains". This is a collection of figures including Batman, Wonder Woman, the Hulk, Teenage Mutant Ninja Turtles, Superman, and others representing the most popular characters from

Marvel and DC Comics. These 41 life size fantasy figures come from the sculpture collection of legendary San Antonio Spurs player Tony Parker, and they will spur memories and delight children and adults of all ages while visiting the museum.

***Admission to this exhibit is FREE with your General Admission to SAMA.

One of the most intriguing items in the museum, dating back to the Egyptian-Roman period of 30 B.C. – 395 A.D, is a cat mummy. This little feline must have belonged to someone special because he was treated to a very elaborate mummification process typically reserved for humans. Because some of the cat's fur was still intact, curators were able to determine that this was an orange tabby cat with a fancy red wrapping on its head.

Come and plan to stay for the day at this very intriguing museum. There are exhibits for the whole family.

200 West Jones Avenue, San Antonio, Tx 78215 210-978-8100 Admission – Adults $20.00, Seniors (65+) $17.00, Military and Students $12.00, youth 13-18 $10.00

Buckhorn Saloon & Texas Ranger Museum

When you come to visit this museum in Downtown San Antonio, you will find it open 365 days a year. Started in 1881 with the private collection of Albert Friedrich, it was originally located on Dolorosa Street. The main attraction in the early days was a 78-point buck that Mr. Friedrich purchased and is still housed in the museum today. To increase the number of horns in his collection, he would offer free drinks to his customers who would bring in a new rack. This collection was known as the "Hall of Horns". Eventually, he was able to add a firearm collection and a mirrored bar which became the saloon that Theodore Roosevelt frequented with his "Rough Riders".

When the saloon was closed during Prohibition the location was moved and re-opened as the Buckhorn Curio Store and Cafe. Once again it moving to the Lone Star Brewery complex in 1956, and finally to its present location on E. Houston Street.

Today, the Buckhorn Museum is filled with birds, fish, and mammals that have been collected from every continent in the world. Over 500 species are represented in this museum.

Within the halls of the Texas Ranger Museum, you will find many artifacts from the Old West including shotguns, pistols, old photographs, and badges. It also features a full-size model of the car that Bonnie and Clyde were driving when they were apprehended and killed, a 1934 Ford V8-Deluxe. Come here to see a jail cell and a blacksmith shop in a model city, fashioned after San Antonio around the year 1900. In addition, you will be introduced to a collection of rattlesnake art and cowboy and American Indian artifacts.

And, if you like a good ghost story, just ask the locals about the several entities that make appearances from time to time, including Billy the Kid. There are even stories of ghostly animals, such as deer and coyotes. Maybe they just want to be featured in the museum along with the 78-point buck.

318 E. Houston Street, San Antonio, Tx. Adults: $22.99 Children 3-11: $16.99

Briscoe Western Art Museum

The Briscoe Western Art Museum holds some of the most interesting and unique items from the earliest days of San Antonio and the Southwest United States. This is truly the area where the West was born. Within this museum, you will be able

45

to learn by examining artifacts and by experiencing history as it evolved from the beginning.

How do we define Western Art?

Western Art brings to life the history and tales of Native Americans, the cowboy, and the vaquero, along with showcasing beautiful sculptures, paintings, drawings, and sketches depicting the vastness and beauty of the scenery of the West.

paintings, and sculptures. As the culture shifts, so does our interpretation of Western art, but the stories remain the same.

There is so much history contained in this building that was originally utilized as the city's public library. It is situated along the edge of the Riverwalk and, in 2013, the dream of former Texas Governor, Dolph Briscoe and his wife, Janey, became a reality. They wanted to fill the museum with the many stories of the heritage of those who lived when the West was won.

There are several dramatic exhibitions that are permanent and if you visit the museum, you will see that it is closed on Tuesdays and Wednesdays but open every holiday of the year except Easter Sunday.

Visiting the permanent exhibits will allow you to see the people, places and things that have formed and are still forming the society of today. The integration of Native Americans, who have been in this territory for many thousands of years, along with the new arrival of immigrants and settlers have formed a new culture, both bold and inventive, existing within the vast and dramatic landscape of the American West.

The artists of the West take their inspiration from spectacular scenes and boundless struggles of both the individual and the collective. As they observe with unending wonder, the infinite subject matter evokes unlimited creativity to be produced in many venues.

As a newcomer to the West and Southwest, the terrain may appear rugged and daunting, some treacherous mountain ranges, desert areas with cactus, lizard and snakes. But to those who have settled in the same region, this is home, with beautiful cactus flowers, wildflowers, snow covered mountains, and land that is to be nurtured and maintained.

The West has a long history of movement. Whether it is the slow movement of the earth as it forces mountains to rise or stretches the plains, it is always changing. As the bison roamed the prairies for ages and the horse was introduced to the continent by the Spaniards to allow hunting and exploration of this vast area, thought of as the Romantic period, it all became inspiration for the artists and craftsmen of the day. This is what Western Art is and it is what you can see at the Briscoe Western Art Museum.

As many museums have a reputation for housing not only their unique artifacts, art, and special cultural objects but also ghosts from the past, the Briscoe Art Museum cannot ignore its special residents. In addition to several that appear from time to time as shadowy figures, roaming throughout the exhibits, there is one specific ghost that we will mention here. John McMullen is his name.

John McMullen was an immigrant who came to the San Antonio area in 1848 and built his home on the site where the museum sits today. He was not very friendly to the neighbors, and it was rumored that he had quite a treasure buried somewhere on his land. In 1853 he was killed in his home in an apparent robbery. Suspicions arose that this terrible murder was committed by his son. The murderer was never found and so this poor soul has been restless ever since.

Although no one can be sure, Mr. McMullen seems to make

himself present in the form of a shadowy figure, with frequent whispers heard, loud banging, and the feeling of being watched. Those who investigate the paranormal have visited this site often and have stated that the basement seems to have the most activity.

210 West Market Street, San Antonio, Tx 78205 210-299-4499 Rating 4.5 General Admission $12.00, Active Duty Military and Dependents $6.00, Seniors and Students 13-18 $10.00

McNay Art Museum

The beautiful Spanish Colonial Revival-style home of Marion Koogler McNay was donated in 1954 and is truly a work of art in and of itself. This 24-room museum was donated to be used for the specific purpose of preserving Ms. McNay's extensive collection of art. When you visit this expansive home, sitting on 23 acres of beautifully manicured lawn decorated with a fishpond, fountains and Japanese-inspired garden, you will be entering the first modern art museum to open in the state of Texas (1954).

Ms. McNay's home was originally built in 1924, as she became the heiress to a large oil fortune from her father.

In addition to this former art teacher and painter's original art collection, over the years galleries have been added that include modernist works from America and Europe as well as art from the Renaissance and medieval periods and a larger collection of 20th-century European and American modernist work.

When she died, this lovely home was left to the City of San Antonio. It houses paintings from famous artists such as Diego Rivera, Paul Gauguin, Henri Matisse, Paul Cezanne, Mary Cassatt, and Pablo Picasso. In all, the museum contains over 20,000 paintings, sketches, and sculptures and over 30,000 volumes in its research library.

A 45,000 square foot addition, designed in the mansion's original architectural style, opened in 2008 to bring attention to many unique exhibits and boasts a lecture hall and learning centers.

If you are wondering if the McNay Art Museum is the home of any ghostly activity, many employees and some visitors have seen the vision of a lady, possibly Ms. McNay, humming and quietly going about her business in her former bedroom, located in the West Wing of the mansion.

6000 North New Braunfels Ave., San Antonio, Tx 78209 210-824-5368 Rating 4.7 Admission- Adult $20.00, Seniors and College Student w/ID $15.00 and Teens 13-19 $10.00

Yturri Edmunds House

The structure standing on this site today is considered to be a house museum and may only be toured by appointment. In the beginning, the land on which this house rests was property of the Mission Concepcion, which is still standing today. When Manuel Yturri Castillo traveled from Spain to Mexico, he became a business owner who eventually became very successful. The government of Mexico, who had control of the land, granted it to Yturri around 1840. His home was built between 1840 and 1860, on this two-thirds of an acre plot of land.

When Yturri's daughter married, her last name changed to Edmunds, and when his granddaughter Ernistine E. Edmunds died in 1961, she willed the property and home to the San Antonio Conservation Society.

This unusual house is a rare structure, built of 18-inch-thick adobe blocks, fashioned from earth, goat hair, and goat's milk.

When the restoration process began in 1964 by SACS, the porch was rebuilt, the home was re-plastered, and the entire interior was restored to its original shape.

The rooms that face the north lie along the Pajalache Acequia, a complex irrigation system built in the 1730's when Spain controlled parts of Texas, to supply Mission Conception and the surrounding farmland with water.

Adjacent to the home, the grist mill was recreated in the 1960s and the Oge Carriage House, originally located in the King William District, was placed on the same acreage. In addition to these buildings, there is another home built of caliche and stone with historical value which was moved from its site on South Flores Street to the Yturi Edmonds House complex. In 1996 this area was added to the National Register of Historic Places in Bexar County, Texas.

128 Mission Road, San Antonio, Tx 78210 210-224-6163 Guided tours are available by appointment only. Minimum of four guest at a cost of $15.00 per person

The O. Henry House Museum

O. Henry was the pen name for a very famous short-story writer whose real name was William Sydney Porter. His most famous work was a story included in most literature books, "The Gift of the Magi". Like many of his short stories, this popular tale features his witty style of writing that includes unique wordplay and unexpected surprises at the end of the story. He led a life filled with adventure (sometimes in a nefarious way) and unfortunately died a broken man with cirrhosis of the liver, complications of diabetes, and heart disease. In spite of his hard-and-fast lifestyle he produced many short stories based on his life experiences. After becoming part of the Buckhorn Museum, his house now rests on the property at Delorosa and

Laredo where it holds furniture from the time that O. Henry lived as well as some of his personal items related to his writings.

601 Dolorosa Street, San Antonio, Tx, 78207

Majestic Theater San Antonio

In all its grandeur, the Majestic Theatre was opened on June 14, 1929. It was purported to be the first Texas theatre to have air conditioning throughout the theatre, which attracted even more visitors, especially in the middle of a hot Texas summer. Its advertisers emphasized that it had "an acre of cool, comfortable seats" and even though it was summer, the letters on the top of the building were covered in snow and fur coats adorned the society ladies attending the opening night.

Even though the theatre was filled to the brim with attendees on opening day, it ironically had to close the next year for several months because of the Great Depression for. But it soon reopened as the average movie-goer attended the movies to avoid the hardship of everyday life. The Majestic was able to thrive during the 1940s and 1950s, providing a much-needed escape through film and live entertainment.

There was no expense spared in the design and decoration of this theatre, from the monstrous cast-iron canopy that covers the sidewalk to the strutting peacock that tops the 76-foot-tall sign in front. The lobby is very large and features murals on the ceiling as well as an aquarium and copper lanterns.

The auditorium is decorated in recreations of sculptures from the Renaissance era, Spanish cypress trees, and other lavish embellishments.

In classic Baroque fashion, the ceiling is designed to have a dark blue cloud effect with its own twinkling stars. These small light bulbs are positioned to reflect the exact location of the stars in the night sky on the opening night of the theatre.

51

Over the years, there have been quite a few world premiers held at the Majestic Theater, including "To Hell and Back" in 1952 starring Audie Murphy in the movie that depicted his life and heroism during World War II. Also, "The Alamo" premiered there in 2004, and Jennifer Lopez attended the premiere of her movie "Selena" there in 1997.

Today, when you attend any live event at the Majestic, you will realize by looking at the lavish décor and architectural design, that this theater holds a very special place in Texas' theatrical history.

Being in the heart of downtown San Antonio makes it very easy to attend one of the many concerts, broadway shows, or live entertainment the Majestic has to offer.

The age of the theater and the many activities that have come and gone in this "majestic" building would lend one to think there may be ghostly residents that refuse to leave these premises. There are a few of these stories that are repeated by the locals.

One ghost story tells of a ballet troupe that came to the theater to perform several times. On their last practice on stage, a heavy stage light fell to the stage floor for no known reason, landing on top of the dancing troupe. Several of the members were killed and, to this day, at times there are shadowy figures seen dancing in the glow of the light bulb stars on the ceiling, perhaps the ballet troupe recreating their last dance.

Another story is recounted by many of the theater staff who have seen the same apparition sitting on the second level, close to the middle of the stage. She appears quite often, sometimes long after the show is over and the curtain is closed for the evening. She is always intently looking toward the stage as if waiting for the show to begin. Staff wonders if she might have been a season ticket holder who is still coming back for more entertainment. She has even been observed by a medium who was attending a live performance.

The employees of the theater have no doubt that the Majestic Theatre is haunted because they have seen too many objects moving by forces that are unseen or apparitions that have appeared on the stage or in the audience. You'll have to investigate for yourself and attend a performance while in town.

224 East Houston Street, San Antonio, Tx 78205 210-226-5700

Rating 4.7

Ticket prices depend on current event

The Aztec Theater

During the early and mid-1920s the economy of the United States was roaring as if nothing could stop it. This theater is a prime example of the lavish, over the top architectural designs the motion picture theaters tried to emulate. The decorations flash with brightly colored furnishings, murals, and sculptures which emulate the artifacts of the Meso-American era.

The lobby of the Aztec theater holds a gigantic chandelier, weighing in at two tons, that was totally refurbished to its former beauty. Ironically, this extravagant piece of art was originally installed in 1929, the very same day of the stock market crash.

This theater enjoyed immense popularity for many decades, but began to decline in the 1970's eventually, eventually falling into ruin and closing in 1989. Ultimately, with the popularity of the RiverWalk and because of its historical value, it avoided demolition and was restored to its past beauty. Today, it is used as a multi-faceted venue for entertainment and for hosting private and public events.

The Empire Theater

THE WILD WEST – That was how San Antonio appeared to the

world in 1877. With the arrival of the railroad, the city eventually moved into an era that brought modernization and conveniences to this ever-growing area.

The new century brought paved roads, the establishment of new universities, and prosperity to San Antonio. At the intersection of St. Mary's Street and Houston Street were a group of buildings that have served as the center of the art community since 1879. Among these establishments was the Empire Opera House. Tragedy struck when the opera house was burned and destroyed. When it was rebuilt in 1913 to become the Empire Theater, it was designed in the style of European theaters, filled with the most modern equipment and projecting a lavish and opulent ambience to attract visitors from near and far. The tall walls of the theater were coated with pounds of gold dust to create an elegant sparkle inside the theater.

When the Empire Theater opened just after World War I began, it was very popular and attracted many famous celebrities such as Mae West and Charlie Chaplin. But unfortunately, in 1921, this theater was dramatically damaged in the great flood of the downtown area and never fully recovered. After World War II, it was billed as an adult film house, along with several other adult businesses on that section of Houston Street, and it closed for business in 1978.

Both the Empire Theater and the Majestic Theater were thankfully saved from demolition by the Las Casas Foundation and its benefactor, Joci Strauss, when, in 1988, a renewal began of the entire downtown area. Today the Empire and Majestic theaters share hallways that meander like tunnels between the two, sharing dressing rooms and some heavy equipment and storage space. They operated together in conjunction with partners (the city and Las Casas) without public funds.

You will find no "off-season" at this theater, so expect great entertainment any time you visit the city.

Like many other old buildings, it is possible that there is one specific ghost that haunts the Empire Theater. Legend has it that back in 1931 a gentleman was waiting to enter the theater for a performance when another man suddenly approached him. The first gentleman appeared to be dressed nicely and project an affluent appearance, while the second man seemed to be dressed in a scruffy manner. The scruffy man grabbed the first man's arm and asked for a quarter, which would have been enough money to buy a ticket to the theater performance. Initially annoyed, the man realized the Great Depression had been cruel to many people, so he reached into his pocket for the money only to look up and realize the scruffy man had disappeared. Even though the scruffy man is not often seen, he does appear occasionally to ask the unaware theater goer for only twenty-five cents. He must be perpetually stuck in this zone around the Empire Theater and unable to leave the place where he asked for money. Keep an eye out for someone dressed in 1930s scruffy clothing, treat him with kindness should you see him, and remember "There but for the grace of God, go I".

10

The Alamodome

B uilt in 1993, this events center started out as the home of the San Antonio Spurs. After 10 years of playing basketball in this arena, the Spurs became unhappy with the facility and required a bigger and better indoor stadium. Bexar County honored this request and built the AT&T Center, which now houses the Spurs.

The Alamodome is located on the southeast perimeter of downtown and, thanks to its proximity to the Alamo, it should come as no surprise that it is also reported to be haunted. Several spectral figures have been seen wandering in the parking lot, with one woman dressed in pioneer clothing, clearly upset and moaning. It has been suggested that her family was killed in that area long ago by merciless enemies. Other entities have been seen floating in the halls of the gigantic structure, possibly just wanting to find a good seat. But a famed medium who visited the Alamodome to investigate said she felt the presence of both male and female ghosts who evidently were floating on the periphery of the Alamodome windows.

While rumors abound, we do not have any hard evidence of

paranormal activity at the Alamodome.

11

San Antonio Sea World

San Anotonio's Sea World has the distinction of being the largest of the Sea World brand parks as well as the largest theme park located in San Antonio. It rests on 250 acres in West San Antonio and serves as the areas only animal theme park, with a focus on animal rescue, conservation of maritime-life, and education.

On opening day, May 27, 1988, there were 75,000 visitors present. 3.3 million visitors came during the first year, making the park one of the Top 10 draws in Texas .

After merging with several different entities over the years and re-vamping their entertainment shows to feature the Orca whales instead of killer whales, SeaWorld Orca Encounter opened in San Antonio.

This SeaWorld has several exciting rides including 3 roller coasters, a kiddie roller coaster, a combination roller coaster and log ride, a three-armed spinning ride, a mini Ferris wheel, and a kiddie drop ride along with a number of others.

You will not be disappointed at the entertainment scattered throughout the park. There are several educational shows featuring dolphins and whales, sea lions and otters, along with an exciting water ski stunt show.

SeaWorld San Antonio has a collection of dolphins (18) and beluga whales (10) that were either rescued or born within a Sea World park. Additionally, there are eight Pacific white-sided dolphins that reside there. Sea otters, green sea turtles, loggerhead turtles, and a variety of fish all live in an exhibit that was introduced in 2019, allowing guests to feed animals for an additional charge. In May 2012, a separate water park opened adjacent to SeaWorld under the name Aquatica.

10500 Sea World Drive, San Antonio, Texas 78251 210-520-4732 Admission Single day ticket $49.99, All day ticket + dining $84.99. Season passes and 12 month passes available.

12

Parks in San Antonio

F riedrich *Wilderness Park*

This park was made possible when a gracious benefactor, Mrs. Norma Friedrich Ward left almost 200 acres of land to the city of San Antonio upon her death in 1971. Her dream was for this land to be used specifically for a public park and to preserve and protect local birds and wildlife along with the native vegetation and trees of the area. Enlargement of this park was complete the following year when another large parcel of land was donated. The park was dedicated for use in 1978.

If you are a bird watcher, this is definitely a park that you want to visit as it provides sanctuary for at least two federally named species of endangered birds: the Black-capped Vireo and the Golden-cheeked Warbler.

Within the park, you can hike over ten miles of trails that entice the beginner or handicapped, and the seasoned hiker with its deep canyons and steep hills. Volunteers provide education on the environment, natural wildlife, and the vegetation of the area.

21395 Milsa Dr, San Antonio, TX 78256
Friedrich Wilderness Park Office: 210-207-3780

Woodlawn Lake Park -

Outside the city limits of San Antonio, in 1887, two men first began to develop 1000 acres of land to become the first development of its kind.

Next, a dam was built to form the 80-acre lake which even had a trolley that ran to the heart of downtown San Antonio to Houston Street. This lake soon became a destination for those requiring such luxuries as the floating dance pavilion.

As time passed and poor financial decisions were made, the lake and surrounding land were leased to a school for boys until 1910. The city of San Antonio acquired ownership of the land in 1918 and, in 1920, a group of businessmen started planning a revitalization project. Many improvements have been made since those early years—streets were paved, 100 trees were planted, and a playground, a jogging track, and community pool were added.

Over the past 100 years this park has become a very popular attraction thanks to the many amenities that have been added. You can fish off the docks, take advantage of the tennis court, enjoy the walking trails, and use the pavilions for family time together.

Since the late 1990s the city's Fourth of July fireworks display and parade have been held here and still draw large crowds each year.

103 Cincinnati St. San Antonio, TX 78201

Hemisfair Park

This historic park and district was originally the area covered by San Antonio's own World's Fair (HemisFair) held in 1968 to celebrate the city's 250th anniversary and the joining of the cultures of the America's with both diversities and similarities. In this district you will find simple homes made of adobe that were constructed in the Spanish and Mexican year of control alongside mansions built toward the end of the 20th century.

When you visit this area you will be able to imagine what life was like in a more simple time, and things like the Acequia Madre (a series of irrigation canals used for watering the surrounding farmland) will make sense as to its importance. Much of this neighborhood was demolished in order to build HemisFair Park, but there were 22 structures that survived, and two were restored and brought back to life.

Today, this park is a favorite for the local residents to enjoy, particularly the wood and sand playground that was built for kids, featuring space tunnels and a castle for their entertainment. The Tower of the Americas was built specifically for the fair, and now stands as a 750-foot-tall part of San Antonio's well-known skyline.

434 Alamo Street, San Antonio, TX

Eisenhower Park

Not surprisingly, this park was named for former President Dwight D. Eisenhower and was originally a part of the army's training grounds near Camp Bullis. Since 1988 it has been open to the public for hiking and outdoor enjoyment. Visitors can enjoy camping, a playground for the younger folks, and nature trails.

The trail system includes over six miles of trails that offer various levels of difficulty. Some trails are paved, providing an easier hike more suited for families taking a leisurely walk. Others are more difficult trails with a natural surface, making for a more challenging trek. In other words, no matter what type of challenge you are up for, you will be able to find a trail to your liking.

At the end of the trail named Cedar Flats Trail you will come upon a look-out point located near the peak of the park. At this look-out, you will be able to see several great views of downtown San Antonio. Keep your eyes out for the local wildlife, which could consist of skunks, raccoons, white-tail deer, and the ever present and interesting armadillos. Bird watchers are also often rewarded by the birds they are able to spot.

While the paved trails are easier to navigate, serious hikers may prefer the natural surface trails found on The Hillview Trail. This is a trail less traveled and borders on a rock quarry which is partially hidden by purposefully planted bushes. Another trail, the Yucca Trail, is partially natural surface and partial pavement. When you get to the end of this trail you will find campsites available to reserve for your overnight stays.

19399 NW Military Hwy., San Antonio, Tx 78257 210-207-7275

Miraflores Park

The lovely name of this park means "look at the flowers" in Spanish. In recent years, this ancient private garden was acquired by the city of San Antonio and gifted a grant for a major renovation. Originally bought in 1914, a highly regarded doctor who came from Mexico planned to build a hospital on 15 acres of land and he called 4 ½ acres of this plot Miraflores.

Unfortunately, the hospital was not built, but this area of land became an obsession of the good doctor as he planned its landscaping and envisioned it becoming a place of beauty and peace so that recovering patients could enjoy it and perhaps speed their recoveries.

His great granddaughter, who was interviewed recently, believes the doctor's passion was rooted in a desire to stay connected to his homeland of Mexico.

As of today, the restoration process has begun and this park, which is now part of Brackenridge Park and located along the Hildebrand Ave. border, will eventually be restored to its original beauty.

Reinforcement and straightening of the towers at the entry gate is currently complete. Restoration of the lanterns has also been completed and the original tiles near the front towers have been removed new tiles are coming from the same region in Mexico as the originals. They are exquisite and brightly colored Mexican Talavera tiles that will add a lovely burst of color to the garden. There are sculptures to enjoy such as the one of Coatlique, the great mother earth goddess, and her daughter, the moon goddess Coyolxauhqui. Somehow over the decades, the head of the mother was moved to rest upon the daughter's body and the head of the daughter now rests upon the mother's body. No one knows how this took place and is a very eerie sight.

This park is intended to be a place to come and enjoy the beauty of the landscape and the solitude it provides to those who want to meditate or reflect on issues in their lives.

Along with the pathway, trees will be added, and original bricks now buried will be used for the new walkways. And there are many unique sculptures and statues like Cuauhtémoc, the fierce warrior and last Emperor of Mexico which was acquired for the garden in 1921.

In 2018, the Miraflores Garden or "Mexican Garden of Memories" was officially opened to the public to enjoy and use as a teaching tool, and to help educate the public on Mexico's history and culture. It can be accessed through Brackenridge Park.

13

Golf Courses in San Antonio

TPC San Antonio
A weekend golf getaway. A family vacation with family and friends with a little golf thrown in. Entertaining clients or customers. These are all easily made possible at TPC San Antonio with close proximity to the San Antonio International Airport. Being adjacent to the JW Marriott San Antonio Hill Country Resort and Spa, where you must stay if you are not a member, makes it super convenient to access one of the two courses, the AT&T Canyons or the AT&T Oaks which was designed by Greg Norman and Sergio Garcia.

Beginning in 2010, the Oaks course has hosted the PGA's Valero Texas Open.

In addition to the 2 challenging 18-hole courses, please find a 23-acre practice area, great instructors suitable for all levels of play, large practice areas, and an awesome clubhouse.

The Quarry Golf Course
This world-renowned golf course was once the site for working families in a community known as "Cementville". It has

become the most sought-after play for the many corporate visitors to the San Antonio area. It was designed in 1993 by Keith Foster and has always been locally owned and operated. The owners make sure that this natural wildlife habitat is maintained in the finest playing condition and will give players an unequaled golf experience.

This course has a unique and interesting history. Originally, the property and the adjacent Quarry Market regions were the workplace and neighborhood for the workers and the plant that produced cement for the area. The Portland Cement product was used to build roads, buildings, and other structures in the state. For generations, this neighborhood was called "Cementville". A visual reminder of the booming days of Cementville, its neighborhoods, and its community is the 200-foot tall smokestacks that dominated the landscape and helped precipitate the growth of San Antonio well into the 20th century. This is truly a golf course with a rich history.

444 East Basse Road, San Antonio, TX 78209 210-824-4500
Green Fees: $39 -$89

14

Bed and Breakfast Accommodations

I*nn on the Riverwalk San Antonio*
This beautiful, century-old Victorian is just a 10-minute walk to all the interesting attractions of downtown San Antonio. It has served many purposes over the years, including a dentist's office, a private residence, and apartments. After being completely renovated in 1990, it has since served as this amazing bed and breakfast, with scenic views from its patio, balconies, and windows. Locally owned and operated by a native San Antonian, this establishment seeks to provide a warm welcome and comfortable accommodations for every guest, with a willingness to answer all questions about the local area and its unique attractions.

129 Woodward Pl., San Antonio, TX, 78204, Phone: 830/225-6333

Noble Inns
Just a few steps from the Alamo and other historic places on the San Antonio Riverwalk, you will find three beautiful bed and breakfast accommodations by the Noble Inns. You will be in the famous King William District, where a short walk will take you

past the lovely mansions of the past. If you are looking for a feeling of romance, you will find it at one of the three properties owned by Noble Inns. Each room will give you a sense of elegant style with unique furniture, indulgent fabrics and wallpaper, and artwork provided by local artists.

The Jackson House, built in 1894, is the first of this group. At present, it is only being rented as a "whole house" experience. With amazing 12-foot ceilings on the first floor of this spacious Victorian-era home, marble bathrooms, and fireplaces with antique mantels complete the exceptional experience for up to 12 guests at a time.

107 Madison Street, San Antonio, TX 78204

Phone:210/223-2353 Reservations: 800/242-2770

The OGE House

This magnificent pre-civil war mansion is just steps away from the popular Riverwalk, and encircled by lush lawns and rose gardens. Offering all the modern luxuries one would need to be comfortable, this amazing bed and breakfast will also convey the feeling of bygone days of beautiful gardens with gazebos and spacious verandas for reflection and relaxation.

209 Washington St., San Antonio, Tx., 78204, Phone:210/223-2353

The Pancoast Carriage House is the smallest of the three and offers a more serene and romantic getaway spot, perfect for honeymooners and more intimate gatherings. It consists of one suite and two rooms, a gas fireplace with antique mantels, and marble bathrooms, and is furnished with the finest in antique furniture.

This trio of unique and beautiful mansions is located in the

King William District, downtown and close to so many of San Antonio's historic spots, and convenient to the city's trolley system which passes by frequently every hour and can transport you to any attraction or event in the area.

202 Washington St., San Antonio, Tx 78204

Phone: 210/223-2353

Arbor House Suites

In the year 1903, this series of four cottage homes was built by a Swiss cabinet maker. He built these Victorian-style houses for himself and his family to live in. Each house features an outside garden area, complete with fountains, tables with attached umbrellas, and plenty of seating to relax and enjoy a delivered continental breakfast. Guests enjoy the location which is just steps away from historic La Villita with all its unique shops and eateries, as well as the Henry B. Gonzales convention center and the rest of downtown.

Each of the 4 cottages has three suites that feature décor and art from many different places that make them unique and fascinating.

109 Arciniega, San Antonio, Tx., 78205,

Phone: 210/ 472-2005

A Yellow Rose Bed & Breakfast

Located in the historic King William District, A Yellow Rose Bed and Breakfast offers a unique stay that caters to its individual guests and their specific needs. Visit this beautifully decorated inn for special treatment and lovely accommodations in the heart of downtown San Antonio.

229 Madison, San Antonio, Tx., 78204, Phone: 210/294-5175

Brackenridge House Bed & Breakfast

This two-story mansion, built in 1901 in the Greek Revival style is located in the King William Historic District in downtown San Antonio. Originally it stood on South Alamo Street, until 1985 when it was placed on rollers and somehow moved to its present location on Madison Street. Several months later the restoration of this home began in earnest. Features such as the beautiful longleaf pine floors were brought back to life and the original columns of the Greek revival style were reinforced. New owners took charge in 2011 and their goal is to offer the same excellent service and accommodations that have made Brackenridge House Bed & Breakfast the top-rated establishment it has been known for in the past. Come here for a taste of Texas hospitality and be pampered in luxurious Victorian surroundings.

230 Madison, San Antonio, Tx., 78204, Phone: 830/271-3442

Bullis House Inn Bed and Breakfast

This lovely mansion was built in neoclassical style between 1906 and 1909 by General John Lapham Bullis who came to San Antonio from New York during the 1800s and was responsible for capturing Geronimo, the fierce Chief of the Apache Indian tribe. If you stay at this inn, you may even see him roaming the halls according to legends of San Antonio.

In 1980 the mansion was restored to its original beauty.

621 Pierce Ave. San Antonio, Tx., 78208 / Phone: 210/223-9426

Rates start at $75 per night

King William Manor - San Antonio

This beautiful B&B is located in the very heart of San Antonio, and just a brisk walk away from the Riverwalk. It was built in 1891 as a Greek Revival mansion and, the property and home were sold several times until 1911 when it was updated and reconstructed into the elegant home it is today.

It is the perfect getaway where you can enjoy the ambiance of the Historic King William District, visit the downtown area, experience local cuisine and nightlife, and then come back to the relaxing spacious gardens and the sparkling pool.

1037 S. Alamo St., San Antonio, Tx., 78210 / Phone: 210/222-0144
Rates start at $89

Bracken Bat Cave

15

Other San Antonio Attractions

Natural Bridge Caverns
This fascinating cavern structure was named for the limestone bridge that was formed when a sinkhole developed underneath a 60-foot natural limestone slab bridge, leaving the formation that is the entryway to the cave.

Conveniently located just north of the city of San Antonio where the Hill Country begins, it will amaze you to explore the biggest cavern in the state of Texas. The pleasant temperature, a constant 70 degrees will be a welcome relief from the outside Texas temperature during most of the year. You will be able to clearly see unusual stalactites and stalagmites along with other interesting geological formations. Tourists can travel at least 180 feet below the entrance, although other areas reach 230 feet into the earth.

On March 27, 1960, four university students from San Antonio made a monumental discovery after seeking permission from the landowner to rappel down into a small cave located on the property. They soon realized that the small cave they thought they were exploring was a 2-mile area now deemed the "North Cavern". After many years of development by the landowner, the cavern was officially opened in July 1964.

Several ancient artifacts have been found during the excavation of some of the trails around the caverns. These items include a human tooth, spearheads, and arrowheads that date back to 5,000 B.C. Over the years, other bones and items were found that indicate early people and possibly animals had used the caverns for shelter.

Within the area surrounding Natural Bridge Cavern, you can choose to visit the Natural Bridge Mining Co. Here you will be able to step back into the 19th century and pan for gold and precious artifacts. You will have a choice of "Arrowhead" bags, "Fossil" bags, or "Gem and Mineral" bags to process through the water and sluice procedure to see if you can uncover any hidden treasure such as emeralds, rose quartz, arrowheads, or fossils. Bags may be purchased on-site starting at $10.

You will also find on the premises the Twisted Climbing course and the Twisted Ropes course where you can show off your courage and your athletic abilities and even challenge others to see who has the most strength and determination to finish first. There is even an area for the young children to take the adventure of a lifetime, through the climbing course and a tyke-sized zip line. Of course, parents accompany them as they build their confidence and have fun.

26495 Natural Bridge Caverns Road, San Antonio, TX., 78266 210-651-6101 Tickets range from $22 to $58.50 depending on the different tours available.

Natural Bridge Wildlife Ranch

This park has been rated as being one of the top 10 safari parks in the United States by USA Today. This is a 450-acre ranch filled with juniper trees and creek beds that provide a respite for over 500 native, endangered and exotic animals. You can enjoy interacting and learning about animals, such as the herd of antelopes and giraffes that could saunter by at any moment. This all can be observed as you take a leisurely drive through the park.

This unforgettable day's adventure holds hours of excitement for adults and children of all ages.

You will go on a Texas Style African Safari, beginning with a self-guided tour around the Walk-A-Bout where you can see lemurs at play, only to end your day at the Safari Camp Grill and a visit to the Safari Sweet Spot for a delicious dessert.

26515 Natural Bridge Caverns Rd. San Antonio, Tx., 78266 Phone: 830-438-7400

Admission: Adults - $28.00 Children - $19.99 Children under 3 - FREE

Bracken Cave

Bats! Bats! Bats! They are everywhere when you visit Bracken Cave, the home of 15 million bats of the Mexican free-tailed variety. Conveniently located just north of San Antonio, this colony of bats is the largest in the world, serving as a maternity colony where the females of this species gather to deliver and raise their offspring. The bats in this cave spend every night devouring such crop pests as corn earworm moths, up to 100 tons every 24 hours during the summer months.

The 1500 acres surrounding the Bracken cave were used as ranch land before the present owners bought this property in 1991. Since then it has been managed as a sanctuary for several endangered birds such as the golden-cheeked warbler.

During the summer months between May and September, you can witness first-hand the spectacular sight as the bats appear at the opening of the cave, set in the magnificent Texas Hill Country, to fly in a whirling tornado, out into the open air to begin their foraging of insects. You must obtain a reservation to see this spectacle.

In the early spring, each year, the females anticipating the birth of their young return to Bracken Cave from Mexico and Central America, while the males of the colony choose to roost in smaller bat communities. By June, most of the pups (baby bats) have been born (in single births) and are nesting, huddled together on the walls of the cave in "creches", where they will stay warm while the mothers are out hunting for food. Amazingly, the mothers can return and find their one baby amid millions of other babies (or pups), by using scent, vocalizations, and spatial memory so that they can nurse them at least twice each night.

In a few weeks, it is time for the young bats to test their flying ability, which is very hazardous, between collisions in mid-air and hitting the cave walls to send them careening to the cave floor where the ever-present population of bat-devouring beetles eagerly await an emergency landing. Of the millions of young that are born each year, only half will survive to join their mothers outside the cave to hunt for insects. When the mothers are still nursing they must consume near their body weight each night to sufficiently nurse their pup, thereby forcing them to emerge from the cave early, almost 3 hours before sundown, creating an impressive display for visitors to Bracken Cave to observe.

26101 FM 3009, San Antonio, Tx., 78266

For Reservations: http://naturalbridgecaverns.com/bracken

batflight/

Government Canyon Natural Area

Situated just north of the City of San Antonio, in the Hill Country, is a wild yet beautiful area that was opened to the public in 2005. It is known for its excellent hiking and biking trails that are suitable for expert hikers and beginners as well.

Dinosaurs were the first known inhabitants of this area dating back over 100 million years. They were brought by the plentiful water source and they left their footprints that can be seen today after an arduous hike to an obscure creek bed.

Millions of years later, from 1860 until just a few years ago, the families that settled here depended on the clear springs to provide water for farming and ranching.

In the 1850s, there was a route laid out through this canyon area to take military supplies to forts in the west. This route was originally known as Joe Johnston Road, but locals referred to it as "government's canyon" and that eventually became the permanent name.

In the 1980s, as San Antonio became more dependent on the aquifer that provided an abundance of water to the area, city and county officials became increasingly concerned with maintaining the safety of the water supply. In 1991 a coalition was formed to buy the property to preserve and protect it from further development. This was the beginning of the development of the Government Canyon State Natural Area.

If you choose to hike the trails in this area, please be on the lookout for raccoons, javelina, deer, snakes, and other commonly seen animals. There are several different endangered spiders and the Golden-cheeked Warbler that can be seen, as well.

There are several special events held throughout the year in the park area. Some of those coming up in the fall of 2022 are:

1. Full Moon Hike – a 2-hour, 3-mile guided tour that takes you through the canyon to view the full moon at its peak.
2. Intro to Hiking – For Women Only – This class is for women who have no experience in hiking but want to learn how to prepare for and enjoy this exciting activity. It's an easy, flat, guided tour with an expert to teach about native plants and point out common animals and endangered birds found here. A presentation follows the hike for those interested in learning more.
3. Hike to the Dinosaur Tracks – This is a 3-hour, guided tour through the Canyon area that spans 6.25 miles. It is a moderately challenging route over a rocky path with slight elevation changes. You will be able to see the dinosaur footprints both from an eye-level perspective and from an elevated position while traversing the Outlook Trail.

Overall, the Government Canyon Natural Area can provide many exciting adventures during your visit. Camping sites are available for a longer stay, over 40 miles of hiking trails are popular for mountain biking, hiking, or trail running, and picnicking and special events and classes are offered as well.

12861 Galm Road, San Antonio, Tx., 78254 / Phone: 210/688-9055

Admission starts at $6 per person

Mitchell Lake Audubon Center

Mitchell Lake is situated within the city limits of San Antonio and has an interesting history, dating back to the 1700s when the Spanish settlers used it to supply water for their cattle. It is one of only two natural lakes formed in the state of Texas. Originally labeled "Lake of the Ducks" because of the vast number of ducks that inhabited the area, it was later renamed Mitchell Lake when the Mitchell family bought the property.

Eventually, after the city of San Antonio bought this area from the Mitchell family in 1901 it was primarily used for waste management and was known for its unpleasant smell and was viewed as "unclean". Fortunately, development plans began to reshape the area as golf courses and parks were added to the area surrounding the lake, and a clean-up and revitalization took place.

Today, Mitchell Lake has been leased by the National Audubon Society and is held up by birdwatchers as a sanctuary for the many rare bird species that inhabit the lake area.

The Mitchell Lake Audubon Center is located in a convenient spot to provide a resting place for almost 99% of the birds that are long-distance travelers, who fly hours and sometimes days over the ocean to arrive on the Texas coast.

Each year, over 4,000 students come to learn all they can about outdoor science and conservation and get hands-on experience bird watching in this wetland habitat.

10750 Pleasanton Road, San Antonio, Tx.,

Please call for memberships or seasonal rates: 210/628-1639

16

Most Popular Haunted Place In San Antonio

Victoria's Black Swan Inn
Perhaps the most intriguing setting for a romance story is the Black Swan Inn which is secluded in a beautifully landscaped 35-acre plot within the city on Salado Creek. It is covered with lush lawns and manicured gardens with natural foliage and oak and pecan trees dating back 100 years. The thickly wooded area around the property protects visitors from the hustle and bustle of the city to provide a calm and serene setting. A unique and private country atmosphere is the perfect venue for any special event, including weddings.

However, this property is also known as one of the most haunted sites in the state of Texas. It has been featured on several television shows such as "Sightings" (December 1996) and "Ghost Adventures" (2013), a series on the Travel Channel. Paranormal investigators were filmed as they did research on this property and the buildings that remain on it from long ago.

The property itself has a history of tragedy, dating back to September 18th, 1842 when the bloody battle of Salado Creek left many Texans and Mexican soldiers wounded and dead. Tied to this event, there have been many sightings of Mexican and Texan soldier apparitions that appear to continue the fight that tragically ended that day. In addition, several young boys who have been innocently fishing in Salado Creek have been terrified by screaming specters chasing them off the property. Often the boys have reported hearing drumming in the far-off distance or a hint of smoke in the air.

Ghosts seem to inhabit almost every corner of the property surrounding the Black Swan Inn but the main concentration of activity seems to occur in and around the main house.

Even though some of the paranormal activity that occurs is the "normal" detection of temperature change, lights flickering on and off, as well as noises and sounds that cannot be explained, there are also scary events that involve spirits that seem to reside there permanently.

Over the years several different families-built structures on the land including homes, barns, and a dairy barn. Of these families, several ghosts inhabit the different buildings. Some are children, who mostly like to play tricks on people as they jump on beds, hide belongings and sometimes bite or hit. Others tend to be more frightening and have been recorded by EVP (electronic voice phenomena – spirit voices seemingly found on electronic devices), shouting "GET OUT"!

After being sold several times over the years, in 1991 the inn was bought by its current owners (the Riveras) who eventually remodeled and restored it to its present lovely condition.

Shortly after purchasing the property, Mrs. Rivera was awakened several nights in a row at 3 a.m. to see a man standing at the foot of her bed, staring at her. His appearance was disturbing and, in an attempt to disrupt his appearance, Mrs.

Rivera re-positioned her bed and the visits no longer occurred. Her daughter began to see the ghost of a man peering into her 2nd story bedroom window on stormy nights. This went on for a while, but then stopped. During the visit from the paranormal investigators who filmed the "Ghost Adventures" episode for the Travel Channel, Mrs. Rivera was able to speak to her deceased mother who had previously died in the house.

In addition to being a venue for weddings, you may also make arrangements for a paranormal experience at the Black Swan Inn. It is associated with the Scientific Paranormal Investigative Research Institute of Texas (S.P.I.R.I.T.).

1006 Holbrook Road, San Antonio, Tx., 78218

Call for venue information: 210/323-8424 Paranormal investigations: $75 per person

17

For the Children

O f course, there are plenty of activities for your children at the theme parks, SeaWorld and Six Flags Fiesta Texas, and the Witte Museum, but there are a few more that may be of interest and are not as frequently advertised. Here are a few:

LEGOLAND Discovery Center

Just inside the Rivercenter Mall and steps away from the Riverwalk downtown, you will find this delightful attraction for kids ages 3 – 10. It has so much to offer that you will want to let them spend all day exploring the 10 different areas of the inside park.

The first thing you will see in LEGOLAND is a spectacular replica of some of the most famous historic landmarks, including the Alamo, the Riverwalk, and the monstrous Tower of the Americas. This mini-city is made of Lego Bricks. Lots of Lego Bricks! In fact, over 1.5 million of them!

This city, called MiniLand is interactive and the kids may be able to spot the Minifigures that are hiding among the famous buildings. In the time it would take someone to drive across the state of Texas 43 times, the team at the Discovery Center worked to put 50,000 bricks together to build the mini-Alamodome. Attending one of the center's workshops can fill you in with expert tips and advice on building your own models.

The 4D Cinema offers movies filled with special Lego characters and thrilling adventures with realistic rain, snow, and wind effects to add to the fun. Three 20–30-minute films are offered at rotating times of the day and your ticket includes all three, so check the schedule when you arrive.

Several rides including the "Journey on a Quest to Rescue the Princess", "Kingdom Quest" and "Merlin's Apprentice" are favorites with kids of all ages. There are a few important safety rules, so be sure to follow them with care. You will see creepy skeletons and curious trolls lurking around corners as you try to save the princess. Then the kids can hop aboard Kingdom Quest to ride to their heart's content and try to have the top score of the day. Finally, Merlin's Apprentice features bewitched carts to pedal through the magic chamber to climb high into the air, and become his next apprentice.

849 E. Commerce Street, Suite 910, San Antonio, Tx., 78205

Admission starts at $18.50 per child (2 rides included)

San Antonio Aquarium

This is the perfect indoor activity for children aged 3-11 as well as the whole family. If the temperature outside is unbearable or it is rainy or cold, visit the San Antonio Aquarium for a whole day of fun-filled adventure.

Your kids will be delighted that they can get up close and personal with some of the many fish and animals in the aquarium. Examples of encounters are kinkajou, lemur, armadillo, grey four-eyed opossum, sloth, octopus, and anteater. The feeding experience can take place with koi, toucan, lorikeets, parakeets, parrots, tortoise, shark, caiman (similar to an alligator), stingray, and iguana. (Some age limits for the children apply to these activities.)

Come and enjoy the day with hands-on, exciting adventures that the San Antonio Aquarium will provide. Enjoy seeing the jellyfish float through the water and feel what it is like to touch a snake in a safe and secure setting.

6320 Bandera Road, San Antonio, Tx., 78238

Phone: 210/310-3210

Adults: $21.95/Children 3-11: $16.95/Seniors, Military, College Students: $19.95

Annual Pass and Memberships Available

The Doseum – San Antonio

This is an adventure for children to learn as they play. There are several learning stations within the building that children are encouraged to experience. The Innovation Station will give them the chance to tinker with tools and gadgets in a space big enough for them to build and create what their imagination allows. By working together with siblings and parents, this station will help the little ones understand and master teamwork.

In the Sensation Studio, they will learn all about light and sound. They can create a light show with different color lights or play with the laser beam as it bounces around on mirrors. There are different activities for different age groups.

2800 Broadway, San Antonio, Tx., 78209

Phone: 210/212-4453

Admission: $14 (1 year and up)

Morgan's Wonderland - Morgan's Inspiration Island

This is not just your ordinary, run-of-the-mill theme park

for kids, but a unique park setting for children of all ages and abilities. In fact, the entire family can enjoy the convenience of 25 special "Ultra-Accessible" rides. A favorite among visitors to the park is the "Carousel" which has wonderful, colorful animals to ride and even special chariots to hold wheelchairs that go up and down as well. There are no bright or flashing lights or jerky movements to disturb those who are sensitive to these elements.

In the Butterfly Playground, you will find playscapes that are wheelchair-accessible, gizmos at ground level, and elements of sensory play that will delight all guests. Also in this playground are "Sway Fun" which will swing you back and forth like a big boat, and "Sand Circle" a giant sandbox with all sorts of gadgets and tools that allow your child's creativity to shine as they build things and play in the sand, and "Music Garden" allows everyone to participate with many different musical instruments such as drums, chimes, and xylophones.

Many other areas in the park are unique and will delight your child. This park is truly a blessing for the San Antonio area and its goal is for everyone to have a good time and feel included in all the special attractions.

5223 David Edwards Drive, San Antonio, Tx., 78233

Phone: 210/495-5888

Admission to Morgan's Wonderland Start at:

Guests with special needs: Free / Children 2 and under: Free / Adults age 18-61: $19 / Children 3-17: $13 / Seniors and Military: $13

Hours and Admission Subject to Change Without Notice

Science Mill (located in Johnson City, 1-hour drive from San Antonio)
This education-based facility is being added because of its

proximity to the city of San Antonio and, if you have older children who might be interested in careers in the science or technology fields, it is the perfect place to explore and learn more about opportunities in these fields with some hands-on experience.

This 1880 historic landmark was originally used as a steam grist mill, whose purpose was to process grain for distribution to the local community and rural area. It served several different purposes over the years, eventually becoming a flour mill that closed its doors in 1980. In the early 2000s, parts of the property were converted into a restaurant and entertainment venue. By 2012, the mill had been purchased and renovated to become the Science Mill, whose goal is to inspire and help educate future leaders in the fields of science and technology.

There are over 50 amazing exhibits housed in the Science Mill. Even the names of the exhibits will spark curiosity and imaginative thoughts from your children. For example, the Axolotl exhibit is very interesting. Why would medical researchers be interested in this little salamander creature that comes from Lake Xochimilco, near Mexico City? Let's ignore the fact that they never acquire adult features during their lifetime but keep larval characteristics like fins and gills their entire life. They also have regenerative properties that allow them to re-grow organs and limbs in three weeks without any scars.

Another popular exhibit demonstrates Aquaponics. In the Aquaponics Greenhouse, your children will learn how the raising of fish (aquaponics) and Hydroponics (growing plants using water instead of soil) have been combined to produce a scientific solution for sustainable farming and healthy food production.

Jurassic Flight 4D is an amazing experience. Once you put on the headset, you will be immersed in a world that existed over 100 million years ago. In real time you will experience a sense of flying over the prehistoric landscape while watching fierce battles between dinosaurs in a world created by paleontologists.

Children (0-2yrs) FREE / Children (3-17) $9.50 / Adults (18-64) $11 / Seniors (over 65) $9 / Military: Half Price (with valid Military ID)

Memberships available

101 LadyBird Lane, Johnson City, Tx., 78636

Kiddie Park – San Antonio

Amazingly, this park was built in 1925 and is still operating as the "Oldest Children's Amusement Park in the Country". Some of the rides are original but have been refurbished and restored, so they don't look like they are almost 100 years old.

The rides include a carousel that was hand-made by the Herschel Spillman Company, the largest and most prolific manufacturer of carousels in the early 1900s. Several examples of their work may be seen in the Henry Ford Museum. Other original rides include the mini-Ferris Wheel, the roller coaster, the car ride, and the helicopter ride. Even pony rides are offered on the weekends. There is an arcade where several old-time carnival games can be played and retro snack foods such as spun cotton candy can be enjoyed.

The park moved from its original location on Broadway to the San Antonio Zoo complex in 2019 when an agreement was reached with the zoo to maintain and lovingly preserve this historic park for future generations to enjoy like many families in the past.

3903 N. St. Mary's St., San Antonio, Tx., 78212

Phone: 210/734-7184 Option 4
Admission: Starting at $14 for unlimited rides

18

Top 7 Hiking Trails

L ocated in Eisenhower Park, the Hillview Nature Trail Loop is considered a moderate challenge for most folks. This popular trail consists of a 2.9-mile hike and takes just over an hour to complete. Open every day of the year, you will find a lot of other folks walking, trail running, and hiking this popular route. All dogs must be leashed at all times. Also located in Eisenhower Park are the Cedar Flats, Red Oak, and Hillview trails which are very popular as well.

19399 NW Military Hwy., San Antonio, Tx., 78257

1. McAllister Park Blue Loop Trail is deemed to be somewhat challenging for the simple matter that it takes a little over 2 hours to complete. Most visitors love this park for its mountain biking, hiking, and birding, and they enjoy it 365 days a year. Some areas of this park allow your dog to be off leash. McAllister Park Loop, also found in this park, is an easy 2.4-mile hike that only requires about 40 minutes to complete. Even though it is popular with runners, off-road bikers, and birdwatchers, you may be able to spend some

alone time during light traffic times of the day. Dogs must always be leashed.

13102 Jones Maltsberger Road, San Antonio, Tx., 78247

1. Main Loop to Restoration Way Trail is located in Friedrich Wilderness Park and is deemed to be a moderate challenge. Along with hiking, this trail is used mainly for birding and trail running. It takes approximately two and a half hours to complete this 5.5-mile route. Unfortunately, dogs are not allowed, leashed or unleashed, on this hiking trail.

One more popular trail in this park is the Main Loop and Juniper Trail. Most visitors find this trail to be an easy route that winds along for 2.5 miles and takes approximately two hours to complete. There are no dogs allowed on this trail which is popular for trail running, birding, and hiking.

21395 Milsa Drive, San Antonio, Tx., 78256

1. In downtown San Antonio in Concepcion Park, you will find San Antonio Mission Trail that winds along the Riverwalk and through the area that is home to the historic missions. In general, this trail is considered easy, but is quite long, taking up to 4 hours to complete its 13.9-mile loop. Leashed dogs are welcome on this trail.

Located in the same park, you will find the San Antonio River Hike which will take almost 2 hours to complete. This fairly easy point-to-point hike is 5.5 miles. It is open 365 days a year and is always a beautiful area to spend time walking, bird watching, or hiking. Your leashed dog is welcome on this trail.

500 Theo Parkway, San Antonio, Tx., 78210

1. Just north of Hardberger Park on Blanco Road, you will find the Salado Greenway Trail, which is an easy, out-and-back, 10.8-mile trail that should take about 3.5 hours to complete. Most visitors find this challenge to be moderate, but well worth the effort. As you explore this trail, you will encounter many others enjoying a day of mountain biking, birding, or hiking.

2. Joe Johnston Route Trail is located in the Government Canyon State Natural Area, just outside of San Antonio, near Helotes, Texas. This trail has become more popular recently as dinosaur footprints were discovered along the rocky, slightly elevated, point-to-point route. It will take you approximately 3.5 hours to hike this 9.3-mile loop. Please do not bring your dog. Sadly, dogs are not allowed on this trail.

12861 Galm Road, San Antonio, Tx., 78254,
    Phone: 210/688-9065

1. Mission Reach Trail in Roosevelt Park at the San Antonio Riverwalk is a great 5.7-mile trail that loops around the west side of the San Antonio River. This easy trail will take under 2 hours to complete, and you will enjoy the experience of seeing many native flora and fauna species such as cactus (blooming in the spring with beautiful cactus flowers), agarita berries, and shady pecan trees. You might even run across a rat snake, garter snake, or red-eared slider turtle looking for shade and water. This trail can be enjoyed in its entirety or in segments if it gets too hot. Be

sure to bring lots of water and sunscreen, as temperatures can rise very quickly in the summer.

331 Roosevelt Ave., San Antonio, Tx., 78210

19

Campgrounds and RV Parks

S an Antonio/Alamo KOA Campground
South Texas is proud to recognize this campground as
one of the best in the area and it was voted "Campground
of the Year" in 2015 by KOA. It does not matter if you want to stay
in one of the top-rated cabins, if you would rather bring a tent
or if you prefer to arrive in your own RV, this campground has
all that is needed to make your getaway the perfect adventure.
You will find yourself only ten minutes from the exciting bustle
of downtown without the need to find parking or hassle with the
traffic of the city. The San Antonio bus system provides pickup
just outside the entrance to the park. With so many attractions
in San Antonio, you will find it to be the perfect setting for
a special couple's rendezvous or destination vacation for the
whole family.

In addition, if you need space for a large church retreat, a family
reunion, or a rally you will find it here where there are over 300
sites to house events of any size. The largest enclosed pavilion,

Frederick Hall, has the capacity to entertain a very large crowd. This spacious campground has been locally owned and operated for over 49 years and the Rohde family's goal is to keep their property updated for a comfortable and pleasant visit for you and your family. They work with local attractions and event promoters to make sure they are able to keep their clientele abreast of all the exciting San Antonio area events.

This campground features special events such as a movie night each week, an annual chili cook-off, and weekly authentic Mexican food meals. Major holidays are celebrated with special family-friendly events.

Some of the recreational opportunities that are available include bike rentals, pedal cart rentals, and a year-round pool. Enjoy amenities such as cable TV, the laundry facility, the pizza parlor, and a chuck wagon breakfast on the premises.

In the mood for some fresh air? There is plenty to be had on the Salado Creek Greenway, a beautiful 5.6-mile trail for hikers and bikers that backs up to the campground. Including Rover in your vacation is a snap here, where he can enjoy the super-sized dog park that encompasses over 4,000 square feet.

602 Gembler Road, San Antonio, TX 78219

For Rates and Reservations: 210/224-9296

Admiralty RV Resort

The Admiralty RV Resort boasts a five-star rating and is only a short drive from most major attractions and events that occur in San Antonio. The goal of this RV Resort is to provide its guests with outstanding service and excellent accommodations and amenities that will make them feel comfortable and at home.

When you arrive for your stay you will see that the grounds are beautifully maintained with abundant shade trees and natural vegetation. In addition to the well-supplied RV sites, you will find a sparkling swimming pool (Jr. Olympic size), immaculate bathrooms, a playground for the kids, a basketball court, a gift shop, and much more. Don't forget to bring your family pet who will enjoy the expansive pet playgrounds.

Convenient shuttle service is available for those wishing to visit SeaWorld and it is only a few steps away from the city bus stop where you can jump on a city bus and head to the downtown area to spend the day.

Mission City RV Park

This RV Park has a mission to make it convenient for guests to enjoy all the adventures that San Antonio has to offer. Conveniently located, it is only minutes away from the Alamo, the historical Missions Trail, the Riverwalk, and many downtown dining establishments. This park has a city bus stop just outside the entrance to the park which makes it super convenient to hop aboard and see the downtown sights.

Find all the park amenities that make it feel just like home. Some of these features are the Texas-sized, big-rig pull-through (up to 90 ft. long), picnic tables at each site, laundry facilities, and a dog park, to name just a few.

1011 Gembler Road, San Antonio, Tx., 78219

Phone: 210/337-6501

Call for Rates and Reservations

20

Surrounding Attractions

Animal World and Snake Farm
From its inception in 1967 until the present day, the San Antonio Snake Farm has consistently been one of the most popular attractions in the area. Local residents and far away visitors have been supporting this unique and unusual farm that features snakes, other reptiles, and exotic animals. Roadside travelers have been enticed to see this remarkable collection which has grown over the years. Then, in 2007, when new owners took possession, the facility transitioned into the Animal World and Snake Farm Zoo. With an accreditation from the Zoological Association of America, the goal of the establishment is to educate, conserve and do research with a specialty in animal husbandry.

In recent years the zoo has been able to expand the living spaces for the animals as well as increase the number of animals to over 500 species. Their lifestyles have improved with the restoration projects that have been completed. Improvement in the environment created for the animals has resulted in a more satisfying human experience.

The mission of the zoo has been to create more programs to improve the visitor's interaction and connections to the animals that will continue far into the future.

What are some of the most interesting animals found in the zoo? Do you like snakes?... Lizards? How about the largest snakes in the world? If you do, then you must pull over to the roadside stop at Animal World and Snake Farm, located on Interstate 35, just north of San Antonio.

Let's first look at this collection of large snakes. The largest on earth consists of the reticulated python, the Burmese python, and the anaconda.

Check out the longest snake on earth, the reticulated python, pushing the record length to 32 feet, 9 and a half inches. They, along with the green anaconda are incredible swimmers and they love to ambush their prey. Their superpower is their sense of smell and they have unique infrared pit organs, both of which help to find food.

550 pounds is the record for the heaviest snake, the green anaconda has also been found to reach over 20 feet long. These are water-loving creatures that have been found to consume fish, crocodiles, and even big cats like Jaguars.

The third largest snake in the world is the Burmese python, which has been known to reach a record-setting 27 feet, with a weight of just over 400 pounds. The superpower of this snake is its constricting ability. It can use this power to squeeze its prey before ingesting it.

Along with the longest and heaviest snakes in the world, the zoo has examples of the most deadly, or venomous.

The Inland Taipan which is found in New Guinea and Australia has been charged with the title of the most deadly snake on earth. Feared in this region of the world, this snake is so fast, that it can strike as many as eight times in a row.

If you see a snake that appears to be polka dotted, run the other way because it could be another most venomous snake, Russell's viper. Living in Asia, it has killed more victims than any other venomous snake known to man.

At the zoo, you can also see the Black Mamba, which comes from Africa, and you will have a hard time outrunning this deadly snake! This snake's superpower is its ability to move quickly and it is known as the fastest land snake on earth. Even though it is called "Black" Mamba, it is actually browner with gray or olive-green shades intermingled. The inside of their mouth happens to be dark black.

In addition to the snake collection, you will be able to see many other amazing and beautiful creatures such as the Clouded Leopard (and her 2 cubs), lemurs, and the cute-as-a-button Fennel Fox.

All of these unusual, magnificent and scary creatures can be found at the Animal World and Snake Farm.

5640 IH 35, New Braunfels, Tx. 78132 Phone: 830/608-9270

Admission: Adults - $19.99/Seniors - $18.99/Military - $18.99/Children - $15.99

Tubing on Texas Rivers

The most popular activity that takes place in the hot Texas summer has to be "floating" the river, otherwise known as "tubing". This is especially true in New Braunfels, just north of San Antonio on Interstate 35, where there is a choice between 2 exciting rivers, the Comal and the Guadalupe. The Guadalupe starts in the Texas Hill Country near Kerrville and runs 230 miles to the Gulf of Mexico, while the Comal is a mere 2.5 miles long, but provides a wonderful tubing experience within a shorter period of time.

Many adventures are waiting in New Braunfels in addition to the tubing experience including canoeing, rafting, kayaking, and paddleboarding. And, after the long hot, Texas summer is over, the sport of fly fishing has become a very popular activity as rainbow trout are released all across the state, including in New Braunfels.

There are many choices for accommodations along the stretch of highway between New Braunfels and Canyon Lake that have a view of the river, including cabins and campground areas. Make sure to contact one of the many River Outfitters who can provide information on river conditions that may affect floating opportunities. They are in business to serve their clients and supply them with information, equipment needs, and shuttle rides to and from the river.

There are a few rules of the river, so be sure to check the city's website to be safe and compliant with regulations.

The Comal River that flows through the middle of downtown New Braunfels is the shortest river in Texas, but some say it is the most fun to float! Rent a tube and take the 2.5-mile ride from Comal Springs all the way to the end of the line where you can be picked up and driven in a cool air-conditioned shuttle back to your car.

Take your pick of several fine "Outfitters" where you can rent a tube, run to the river and jump in for a whole day of floating and swimming in the crystal clear river. This water sport is fun for the whole family. Just be sure to check all the rules to be sure everyone stays safe.

The typical cost to float the Comal River is $15 - $22 per person (must be 4 years or older)

Gruene Hall

Located in Gruene Historic District, Gruene Hall is recognized as the oldest dance hall in continuous use in Texas and attracts international visitors from all corners of the world. It was originally built in 1878 and the building and layout have not been altered much over the years. This 6,000-square-foot establishment hosts a bar, the dance floor, and a small stage in the back which has been the launch pad for many hugely popular country artists and bands. Musicians such as Willie Nelson, Garth Brooks, Lyle Lovett, and George Strait have performed on this stage. This historic district has several sights worth seeing, such as the Gristmill restaurant, the Gruene Coffee Haus, the Gruene General Store, and the Gruene Antique Company. This side trip is perfect as an addition to your tubing experience in New Braunfels.

Landa Park

This large, beautiful park is located along the river on 51 acres and provides a variety of activities for all ages to enjoy. Since 1898, Landa Park has hosted visitors, both local and from far away, to spend the day paddle boating, swimming, fishing, and picnicking under the shady oak trees. With two spectacular hiking trails, tennis courts, miniature golf, a regulation golf course, and a miniature train that crosses the whole expanse of the park, there is fun for the whole family.

<u>164 Landa Park Dr, New Braunfels, TX 78130, Phone: 830-221-4350</u>

Schlitterbahn Waterpark Resort

For the last 15 years, this park has been recognized as the BEST waterpark in the world. Its water is fed directly from the Comal River and its expansive 65 acres host many attractions that are expanded every year to provide fun and excitement for the whole family. There are several eateries to experience, but feel free to bring your picnic lunches. Only alcohol is forbidden.

400 N Liberty Ave, New Braunfels, TX 78130, Phone: 830-625-2351

Stars and Stripes Drive-In Theater

You will think you have traveled back in time to the 1960s when you take the family to the drive-in movie on a warm, clear summer night in Texas.

Every night is double-feature night, so come prepared with lots of snacks or enjoy the burgers, corndogs, and other menu items in the throw-back to the 50s-60s cafe. Purchase tickets online or at the theater. Open every Friday thru Sunday, all year round.

1178 Kroesche Ln, New Braunfels, Tx., 78130

Phone: 830-620-7469 (SHOW) | 830/626-1956 Office

Otto's Cheese Shop

This locally owned and operated cheese shop and charcuterie have everything you might want in terms of a delightful dining experience. Their cheeses come from all around the world. The employees are very helpful in determining exactly what would satisfy your tastebuds. Throw in a special beer or enjoy their growing selection of wines to top off your evening.

Pantry items include jams, jellies, canned fish, jars of honey, chocolates, and even Wine chips. Drop in today and have an amazing experience at the "Biggest Little Cheese Shop in Texas".

344 Landa Street, New Braunfels, Texas 78130 Phone: 830/387.4495

21

True Life Ghost Story

Before we end our book, we would like to recount this story from a close relative who lives in San Antonio.

Picture this. A beautiful brand-new neighborhood in Northwest San Antonio, near a newly developed golf resort. Quiet streets. Spacious yards that host deer that wander up to feast on acorns, grasses, or pretty shrubs. This picturesque setting seems idyllic to the casual passer-by, but what is happening inside the house?

Strange things...weird noises...pets acting unusual... Could it be this development was built upon a long-ago and forgotten cemetery, or was it the scene of a battle around San Antonio where soldiers, Native Americans, or settlers fighting for territory died and are still trying to find their final resting place?

It is often said that animals have sharper senses than humans, and can hone in on phenomena that their human owners cannot. This is what happened in the beginning.

Soon after Chuck and Nancy moved into their new home with their daughter, Angie, things gradually began to occur. Angie's bedroom was upstairs, and her little dog began acting strangely. First, she would stand on the bed and stare at the doorway, and then she would bark incessantly when nothing was there. Weird things went on for some time until Angie began to feel uncomfortable and eventually did not want to sleep in that room any longer.

Around the same time this happened, even though Angie would be visiting a friend over the weekend, Chuck and Nancy would hear someone moving around in Angie's bedroom, which was directly above their room. The sound was unmistakable. Footsteps when no one was there.

On a dark, rainy early morning soon after, Nancy was sitting on the bed, and Chuck was in the shower. Suddenly, Nancy was almost knocked off the bed by an unseen force. It was as if a brick had fallen from the ceiling and landed on the other side of the bed. As she abruptly looked over, there was nothing to be seen! At this point, the couple decided they must act against the unknown visitor or visitors that had invaded their home.

At first, the Catholic Church was called but did not offer any solutions. Then, a friend suggested a woman in the city known for "cleansing" homes of bad energy and unwanted spirits. When she came, she discovered three presences in the house. Two spirits were Native Americans or soldiers who had died on the property hundreds of years ago and had been disturbed when construction began in the area. These two spirits were well-behaved and had never caused any trouble until a more aggressive being was brought in unbeknownst to Chuck, presumably after attending a funeral.

After the "cleansing" (with the burning of sage) was complete, the negative energy was gone, and the spirits were never brought forth again.

All is well in the neighborhood! Just look at those pretty deer.

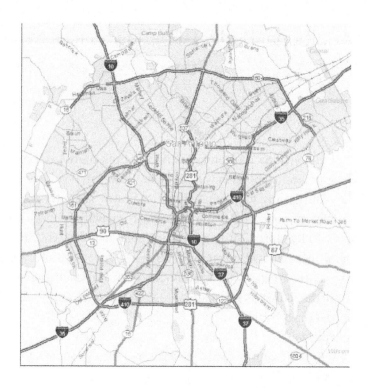

22

Additional Budget-Friendly Places to Stay

I f you visit San Antonio during the peak tourist season, hotels and motels may be booked. However, if you don't mind driving 30 minutes from Downtown San Antonio on Interstate 37, you will find the charming town with the magical name of Pleasanton. It is a pleasant area, and you will find several more budget-friendly hotels with very good overall ratings. Here are the hotels you should check out. (even though some of the addresses say "Jourdanton," these towns are located just next to each other:

Microtel Inn
1311 Brush Country Lane, Pleasanton, Tx., 78064 Phone: 830/268-5057
Rates start at: $74
Savannah Suites
910 Palmer Lane, Pleasanton, Tx., 78064 Phone: 830/569-8100
Rates start at: $51.00
Holiday Inn Express
350 Medical Drive, Jourdanton, Tx., 78026 Phone: 830/769-3323

Rates start at: $117

La Quinta Inn by Wyndham
110 Bmt Drive, Jourdanton, Tx., 78026 Phone: 830/769-3050
Rates start at: $95.00
Hampton Inn
2057 W. Oaklawn Rd., Pleasanton, Tx.. Phone: 830/569-3001
Rates start at: $127.00

23

Conclusion and Please Leave a Review

We hope you have enjoyed this book and are able to plan a trip to the San Antonio area soon. As independent authors with a small marketing budget, reviews are our livelihood on this platform. If you enjoyed this book, we'd really appreciate it if you would leave your honest feedback. We love hearing from our readers, and we personally read every review.

Hey there, adventurous reader! You've just embarked on a budget-friendly journey through San Antonio in our book. Your thoughts matter, and sharing them in a review can help fellow travelers discover the wonders of this guide. Please take a moment to share your honest review at the following link:

https://www.amazon.com/review/create-review/ ref=dpx_acr_wr_link?asin=B0BK1NDCRR

24

Resources:

h ttps://www.thealamo.org/
https://www.nps.gov/saan/index.htm
https://www.sanantonio.gov/
https://www.texasbb.org/?gclid=CjwKCAjws—ZBhAXEiwAv
-RNL9ICrUT4fAwVxZ2h1zRcpYJoe9UM1jz64v1D1RkcyAUOTe
C4NWMUUBoC_h4QAvD_BwE
https://www.visitsanantonio.com/downtown/
https://ghostcitytours.com/san-antonio/haunted-places/h
aunted-hotels/
https://www.brackenridgepark.org/
https://sazoo.org/
https://www.awsfzoo.com/
https://naturalbridgecaverns.com/
https://comaltubes.com/
https://www.batcon.org/see-bats-live/visit-bracken-cave-
preserve/
https://tpwd.texas.gov/huntwild/wild/species/bats/bat-wat
ching-sites/bracken-cave-preserve.phtml
https://seaworld.com/san-antonio/?gclid=CjwKCAjws—ZB

SAN ANTONIO ADVENTURE GUIDE

hAXEiwAv-RNLwFxgeV6TO3Z8vGy8XGrvUl2WIa7nEC9PUkm
6CrjDcOQpZiV82nGwxoC9XYQAvD_BwE&gclsrc=aw.ds
https://www.playinnewbraunfels.com/?gclid=CjwKCAjws—
ZBhAXEiwAv-RNL3dFB3U1a1XQemu4Z1DWz7wRb9-MJpJz_1
MWscaiQubo8iFpIulZ_BoC3nkQAvD_BwE

Made in the USA
Las Vegas, NV
11 April 2024